In and Around London

W A L K S

Compiled by
Brian Conduit

JARROLD

Ordnance
Survey

Acknowledgements
My thanks for the valuable advice and numerous useful
leaflets that I have obtained from Surrey County Council,
the London Walking Forum, Hainault Forest Country Park,
Bromley Council, Ewell Library and the various tourist
information centres throughout the area.

Text:	Brian Conduit
Photography:	Brian Conduit and Jarrold Publishing
Editor:	Geoffrey Sutton
Designers:	Brian Skinner, Doug Whitworth
Mapping:	Heather Pearson, Tina Shaw

Series Consultant: Brian Conduit

Jarrold Publishing   ISBN 0-7117-1055-4

First published 1999
by Jarrold Publishing and Ordnance Survey

Printed in Great Britain
by Jarrold Book Printing, Thetford 1/99

Jarrold Publishing
Whitefriars, Norwich NR3 1TR
Ordnance Survey
Romsey Road, Southampton SO16 4GU

Front cover: The Grand Union Canal near Regent's Park
Previous page: Big Ben and the statue of Boudicca

Contents

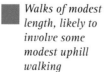

Short, easy walks

Walks of modest length, likely to involve some modest uphill walking

More challenging walks which may be longer and/or over more rugged terrain, often with some stiff climbs

Keymap 1

ST. ALBANS • A414 • Colney Heath • M10 • Water End • South Mimms

HEMEL HEMPSTEAD • Bovingdon • Kings Langley • Chipperfield • Chiswell Green • Abbots Langley • Bricket Wood • RADLETT • Shenley • Shenleybury • Ridge

CHESHAM • Flaunden • Bucks Hill • Chandler's Cross • Chenies • WATFORD • Cassiobury Park • Croxley Green • BUSHEY • Bushey Heath • Elstree • BOREHAMWOOD • Arkley

Little Chalfont • CHORLEYWOOD • RICKMANSWORTH • Heronsgate • Horn Hill • Maple Cross • South Oxhey • Eastbury • Hatch End • STANMORE • EDGWARE • Mill • A1 • M1

Chalfont St. Giles • Chalfont Common • Jordans • Chalfont St. Peter • Harefield • NORTHWOOD • 20 • PINNER • HARROW • Wealdstone • Greenhill • KENTON • Kingsbury • A406

GERRARDS CROSS • Denham • 25 • Ruislip Common • RUISLIP • Eastcote • Harrow on the Hill • NORTHOLT • 6 • WEMBLEY • WILLESDEN • Harlesden • PADDINGTON

Fulmer • Iver Heath • Stoke Poges • Ickenham • UXBRIDGE • HILLINGDON • GREENFORD • Perivale • EALING • ACTON • HAMMERSMITH

SLOUGH • Langley • Iver • Cowley • YIEWSLEY • HAYES • SOUTHALL • Norwood Green • 9 • BRENTFORD • CHISWICK • FULHAM • BARNES

WEST DRAYTON • Sipson • Longford • Cranford • Heston • Osterley Park • Kew Bridge • Kew • A316 • Mortlake • PUTNEY • 8

Datchet • Colnbrook • Poyle • Horton • Wraysbury • London (Heathrow) Airport • Stanwell • HOUNSLOW • ISLEWORTH • RICHMOND • 11 • Richmond Park • Roehampton • WIMBLEDON

WINDSOR • GREAT PARK • Old Windsor • Hythe • STAINES • East Bedfont • FELTHAM • A316 • TWICKENHAM • Ham • TEDDINGTON • KINGSTON UPON THAMES

Englefield Green • EGHAM • ASHFORD • Hanworth • Bushy Park • Hampton Court • 14 • SURBITON • NEW MALDEN

Sunningdale • Virginia Water • Lyne • Thorpe • Littleton • SUNBURY • Laleham • Hampton • East Molesey • Thames Ditton • Long Ditton • Tolworth • Worcester Park • A240

Chobham Common • Shepperton • CHERTSEY • WALTON-ON-THAMES • Hersham • ESHER • Hook • Chessington • 26 • EWELL

M3 • Lightwater • West End • Horsell • ADDLESTONE • Ottershaw • Burrowhill • WEYBRIDGE • Whiteley Village • Esher Common • 24 • Claygate • A243 • Oxshott • EPSOM • Epsom Downs

Bisley • Knaphill • Brookwood • Chobham • Woodham • Byfleet • Wisley • Cobham • Stoke D'Abernon • A245 • Ashtead • Tadworth

Pirbright • WOKING • Pyrford • M25 • LEATHERHEAD • Fetcham • Headley

SCALE 1:250 000 or 1 INCH to 4 MILES *1CM to 2.5KM*

0   2   4   6   8   10   15   KILOMETRES

0   2   4   6   8   10   MILES

KEYMAP HEIGHTS SHOWN IN FEET

Worplesdon • Pitch Place • Stoughton • West Clandon • East Clandon • Great Bookham • Mickleham • Westhumble

Normandy • A323 • East Horsley • Effingham • Buckland

See Keymap 2, page 6

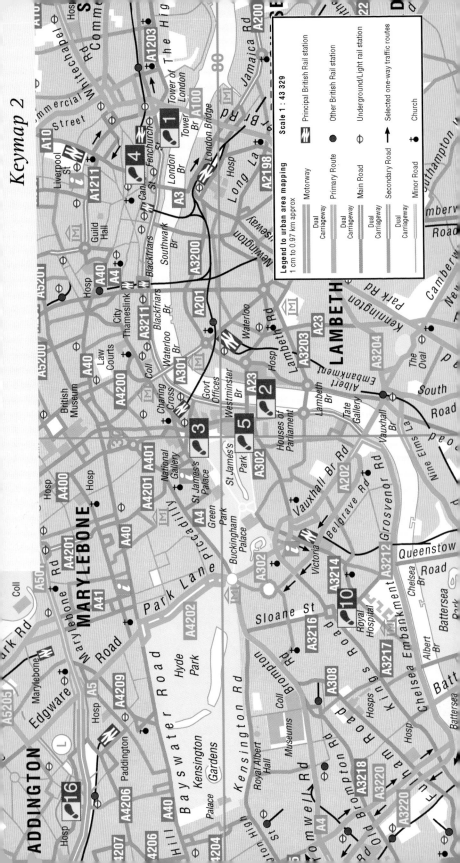

Keymap 2

Legend to urban area mapping
1 cm to 0.97 km approx

Motorway		Dual Carriageway
Primary Route		Dual Carriageway
Main Road		Dual Carriageway
Secondary Road		Dual Carriageway
Minor Road		

Scale 1: 43 329

🚉 Principal British Rail station
● Other British Rail station
Φ Underground/Light rail station
↑ Selected one-way traffic routes
✝ Church

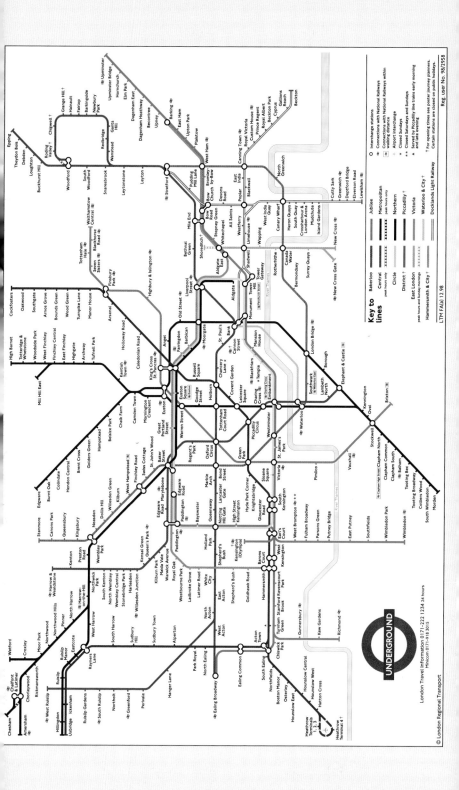

Walk	Page	Start	Distance	Time
Banstead Wood and Park Downs	60	Chipstead, Holly Lane	4½ miles (7.2km)	2 hrs
Biggin Hill	71	Biggin Hill, recreation ground	6½ miles (10.5km)	3 hrs
Blackheath and Greenwich Park	44	Blackheath Station	5 miles (8km)	2½ hrs
Cassiobury Park and Whippendell Wood	65	Watford, Gade Avenue	6 miles (9.7km)	3 hrs
Chelsea and Battersea Park	36	Chelsea, Sloane Square	4 miles (6.4km)	2 hrs
City of London, Through the	22	Monument	3½ miles (5.6km)	2 hrs
Colne Valley, South Harefield and Bayhurst Wood	77	Denham Country Park	7 miles (11.3km)	3½ hrs
Cudham and Downe	87	High Elms Country Park	8 miles (12.9km)	4 hrs
Enfield Chase	50	Trent Country Park	4 miles (6.4km)	2 hrs
Epping Forest	68	Epping Forest Museum, Chingford	6 miles (9.7km)	3 hrs
Esher Common, Oxshott Heath and West End Common	74	West End Common, Esher	7 miles (11.3km)	3½ hrs
Farthing Downs and Happy Valley	84	Farthing Downs, Coulsdon South	8 miles (12.9km)	4 hrs
Hainault Forest	55	Hainault Forest Country Park	5 miles (8km)	2½ hrs
Hampstead Heath	41	Hampstead Station	4½ miles (7.2km)	2 hrs
Hampton Court and Bushy parks	47	Hampton Court Station	5½ miles (8.9km)	2½ hrs
Horsenden Hill	28	Horsenden Lane	2½ miles (4km)	1½ hrs
Little Venice, Regent's Park and Primrose Hill	52	Little Venice	5½ miles (8.9km)	3 hrs
London's Docklands, Through	14	Tower of London	3 miles (4.8km)	1½ hrs
Marden Park Woods	58	Woldingham Station	4½ miles (7.2km)	2 hrs
Nonsuch Park and the Hogsmill River	80	Ewell West Station	8½ miles (13.7km)	4½ hrs
Osterley Park and the Grand Union Canal	34	Osterley Park	4½ miles (7.2km)	2½ hrs
Parkland Walk from Finsbury Park to Highgate	30	Finsbury Park Station	3½ miles (5.6km)	2 hrs
Royal parks and palaces of Central London	25	Parliament Square	4 miles (6.4km)	2 hrs
Ruislip Woods and Lido	62	Ruislip Lido	5½ miles (8.9km)	3 hrs
South Bank of the River Thames, Along the	17	Westminster Bridge	3 miles (4.8km)	1½ hrs
Thames from Richmond to Kew, Along the	38	Richmond Station	5 miles (8km)	2½ hrs
West End – St James, Mayfair and Piccadilly	20	Trafalgar Square	3½ miles (5.6km)	2 hrs
Wimbledon Common	32	Wimbledon Common Windmill	3½ miles (5.6km)	1½ hrs

Comments

There are many fine wooded stretches and a sense of remoteness on this walk on the North Downs.

The walk passes through several fine wooded areas, and there are extensive views across the North Downs to the Kent Weald.

The circuit of Greenwich Park, with its rich assortment of grand buildings, beautiful gardens and fine views over the Thames, is especially memorable.

A combination of parkland, woodland and waterway walking beside the River Gade and Grand Union Canal makes for a most satisfying and varied walk.

The varied architectural attractions of Chelsea on the north side of the Thames contrast with the more rural pleasures of Battersea Park on the south side of the river.

A series of Wren churches are passed – including St Paul's – plus aspects of the City's legal, financial, commercial and administrative heritage.

Pleasant canal walking and some delightful woodlands are combined with a visit to an attractive old church.

From a most attractive starting point, the route passes through some delightful woodland, two villages – with medieval churches – and the house in which Charles Darwin lived and worked.

This is a pleasant figure-of-eight walk through the woodlands and across the grassland of Trent Country Park, one of the few remaining areas of Enfield Chase.

The dense woodlands and open grasslands of Epping Forest, an invaluable recreational amenity on the east side of London, are among the finest in the country.

This figure-of-eight walk explores three adjacent commons, which make up one of the largest remaining areas of heathland within the circumference of the M25.

This walk offers grand views across the downs, superb woodlands and an isolated and attractive medieval church.

Despite the proximity of north-east London, there are some grand views over the Essex countryside and some splendid areas of woodland.

The nearest real country walk to the centre of London, across rough heath and through woodland, that includes an 18th-century mansion and a fine viewpoint.

An invigorating walk across parkland and beside the Thames that has the magnificent Hampton Court Palace as its chief focal point.

Wooded slopes, a fine viewpoint, meadowland and a peaceful stretch of the Grand Union Canal make up a surprisingly rural walk in the heart of suburban west London.

A highly attractive stretch of the Regent's Canal is followed by a circuit of Regent's Park and a short and easy climb to the superb viewpoint of Primrose Hill.

A fascinating walk from the grim medieval walls of the Tower of London to the ultra-modern Canary Wharf complex, which reveals some of the vast changes in this former Dockland area.

A series of delightful woodlands and extensive views across the North Downs are the chief ingredients of this walk.

A circuit of Nonsuch Park, site of a now vanished palace built by Henry VIII, is followed by a ramble along the banks of the Hogsmill River.

From the rural surroundings of Osterley Park and its great house, the route follows a stretch of the Grand Union Canal through the Brent River Park, passing one of Brunel's engineering triumphs.

Most of the route follows a disused railway track through north London, finishing with a stroll through two adjacent and attractive woods.

A series of parks and palaces are linked on a green walk in the heart of London – a walk steeped in English tradition, pageantry and history.

The beautiful Ruislip Woods, remnants of the old forest of Middlesex, provide enjoyable walking in a largely suburban area.

This walk along the South Bank includes views of the Houses of Parliament and St Paul's and passes the South Bank Arts Complex, Clink Prison Museum and Southwark Cathedral.

An attractive stretch of the Thames Path is followed from Richmond downstream to Strand on the Green and Kew, with a chance to visit the world-famous Kew Gardens.

A relaxing walk that leads you through the most stylish and elegant parts of the West End.

The wide expanses of grassland and delightful wooded areas on Wimbledon Common provide pleasant and easy walking.

At-a-glance...

Introduction to
In and Around London

The walks in this guide are all within the circumference of the M25 motorway. They make up an unusually varied collection, and many people, both
Londoners themselves and visitors to the capital, may well be surprised by
how much open, attractive and unspoilt countryside still survives in an
area that is often considered to comprise little more than sprawling suburbs
and congested roads with little to offer walkers.

The walks fall into three main categories – urban, suburban and rural –
although the distinction between them can sometimes be a little blurred.
There are walks in the very heart of London – through the City, West End,
Westminster, Docklands, Chelsea – mainly using a combination of roads,
riverside promenades and parks. Some walks take you through oases or
narrow fingers of greenery in predominantly suburban areas – Horsenden
Hill, Ruislip Woods and the Brent River Park are three such examples –
that either managed to survive, or have been reclaimed from, the rapid
expansion of housing, roads and industry that occurred particularly in the
1930s. The remainder of the walks are in the rural fringes just beyond the
boundaries of the capital – Epping Forest and Enfield Chase, the Surrey
heathlands and North Downs. Many of these have an unexpected solitude
and tranquillity normally experienced only in the more thinly populated
and remote parts of Britain and give the impression that both the M25 and
London's suburbs are hundreds of miles away.

Urban walks

In many respects London is a walker's city. Because of its huge variety of
attractions and large surviving areas of greenery, the city has much to
interest those who particularly like to combine their recreational walking
with some sightseeing. As one of the world's great capitals, London has an
almost infinite number of sites and buildings of major architectural and
historic interest, so the urban walks have been planned to link as many of
these sites as possible and to allow plenty of time for visits. This is why
they are all reasonably short. There will also be time perhaps to call into
some of the numerous restaurants, coffee shops and in particular the
traditional pubs – many of these of great historic interest in themselves –
that are passed *en route*: all part of the experience and enjoyment of
walking in Central London.

Many have remarked that London's chief glory – and the one that sets it
apart from most other European capitals – is its splendid expanses of
parkland. Foremost of these are the four adjacent royal parks of St James's,
Green, Hyde and Kensington Gardens, which cut a huge green swathe

across the very heart of the capital. Most of them were originally enclosed by Henry VIII as deer parks, and they have been open to the public since at least the reign of Charles II. A little further away is Regent's Park, also enclosed by Henry VIII but created in its present form by John Nash, with the support and encouragement of the Prince Regent. At Greenwich to the east is the oldest of the royal parks, while to the west are the adjacent parks of Hampton Court and Bushy and the largest of them all at Richmond. In addition, there are other parks and open spaces – large and small – ranging from the wild and hilly expanses of Hampstead Heath and the grassland and woodland of Wimbledon Common, to the traditional ornamental gardens of Battersea Park. Even amidst the bustle of the square mile of the City, there are peaceful little enclaves, like the Temple Gardens and Postman's Park, where you can escape from the crowds and the noise of the traffic.

Many of the urban and suburban walks make use of the Thames Path, a National Trail that follows England's best-known river from source to mouth. The London section of it enables people to enjoy attractive walks, from Richmond in the west to Greenwich in the east, mainly along traffic-free riverside paths and embankments on both sides of the river. The Thames has always been a major artery – and the easiest form of travel in the past - which is why so many royal and other palaces were built near its banks. In the heart of London, some of the finest and most dramatic skylines are to be seen from the Thames Path, as well as many of the city's major landmarks and tourist attractions.

Suburban walks

At first glance suburban London might not sound promising territory for walking as it lacks the rural appeal of the green belt and the historic

Osterley Park – a great house and estate in Greater London

and architectural attractions of the urban walks. However, there are many varied and satisfying walks to be sampled here. Riverside meadows by some of London's lesser-known rivers – the Colne, Lee, Pinn and Brent – provide pleasant walking, and some sizeable remnants of the forests that once surrounded London still survive

Introduction

amidst the suburban housing, preserving something of the pastoral landscape of 'Rural Middlesex', whose destruction was so much lamented by John Betjeman, the poet of suburbia.

Several walks make use of the Grand Union Canal, which starts its journey to Birmingham in the heart of London at the back of Paddington station. From here it winds its way through the western and north-western suburbs, before continuing into the more open Hertfordshire countryside.

One attractive feature that walkers in London will soon realise is the extent to which some of the small towns and villages that have been engulfed by the city's growth retain something of their former rural atmosphere, with large greens where cricket is still sometimes played, traditional pubs, picturesque cottages and old churches. Hampstead, Blackheath, Wimbledon and parts of Chelsea immediately spring to mind, and further westwards along the Thames, Kew and Richmond still remind us that they were once quiet riverside settlements.

Rural walks

Beyond the suburbs but still within the M25 there is a relatively narrow rural area, within which a surprising amount of open countryside remains. In the Middle Ages, London was surrounded on all sides by huge expanses of thick forest and rough heath, and there are still quite substantial remains of these. Of the once vast forest of Essex, Epping and Hainault provide excellent walking facilities, and fragments of the old Forest of Middlesex survive at Enfield Chase and Ruislip Woods.

Some of the finest and most unspoilt country near the capital is to be found on the North Downs in Surrey and Kent. From the well-wooded downland slopes, the views often extend from the Thames Basin to the lush and silvan pastures of the Weald. In western Surrey, areas of the rough and

Horse Guards Parade

A view of the Marden valley

inhospitable heathland, once so detested and feared by travellers, still survive amidst the affluence and large houses of Esher and Oxshott.

For the preservation of at least some of these rural landscapes - both as segments of unspoilt countryside and as places for public recreation and enjoyment – we have to thank the Corporation of the City of London, who have protected them from development since Victorian times. Two such areas are Epping Forest and Farthing Downs just to the south of Croydon. Two regional parks based on rivers – the Colne in west London and the Lee in east London – have been established to preserve and enhance the rural landscape of those valleys and provide a range of recreational amenities.

Walking in the area

Apart from the Thames Path, there are a number of other well-waymarked routes in and around London. Many of the walks make use of stretches of the London Loop, a 150-mile (241km) route that will ultimately encircle the capital, passing through some of the finest rural areas of the Home Counties. 'Loop' stands for London Outer Orbital Path and, when completed, it will be the walker's equivalent of the M25. A 72-mile (116km) inner orbital route – the Capital Ring – is due to follow soon, and both are connected to the 1243-mile (2000km) London Walks Network, which is being developed by the London Walking Forum.

These initiatives will only add to the already extensive network of attractive and well-waymarked routes already available to walkers both within and around Britain's capital city.

Through London's Docklands

Start	Tower of London
Finish	Canary Wharf
Distance	3 miles (4.8km)
Approximate time	1½ hours
Refreshments	Café at the Tower of London; plenty of pubs, restaurants and cafés at both the St Katharine Docks and Canary Wharf; some interesting East End pubs at Wapping and Limehouse
Public transport	Underground to Tower Hill (District and Circle lines; Docklands Light Rail from Tower Gateway), return on Docklands Light Rail from Canary Wharf
Ordnance Survey maps	Landranger 177 (East London, Billericay & Gravesend), Explorer 173 (London North, Harrow & Enfield)

The walk takes you through the heart of what, in Victorian times, was the busiest and most extensive port in the world. The docks are no more, and now the area is a fascinating mixture of old and new, with traditional riverside pubs and old churches surviving among refurbished 19th-century warehouses, fashionable marinas and giant new developments. The starting and finishing points themselves vividly illustrate these contrasts. You begin by the medieval walls of the Tower of London and the Victorian grandeur of Tower Bridge, and end at the striking, new and enormous Canary Wharf complex.

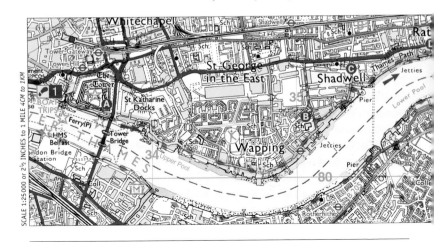

Note that at times building developments may necessitate diversions where the Thames Path leaves the road and runs beside the river. All such diversions will be clearly marked and in most cases will simply require you to continue along the road.

A path leads under the road from Tower Hill Station to the west side of the Tower of London. Turn right alongside the former moat, follow the walls round to the left and, in front of the ticket office, turn right up to an open area. Turn left, go through gates into the precincts of the Tower and turn left on to a path that runs between the river and the walls of the Tower.

The Tower of London and Tower Bridge are two of the most familiar landmarks in the capital. The much restored White Tower survives from the original castle, built in the late 11th century by William the Conqueror to overawe and defend the capital. It stands at the heart of a huge fortress, enlarged and modernised by successive monarchs, which has served as a palace, barracks, prison and place of execution. Among the many and varied people who have suffered incarceration or execution – or both – within its grim precincts are Edward V and his brother (the Princes in the Tower), two of Henry VIII's wives (Anne Boleyn and Catherine Howard), Lady Jane Grey, Sir Thomas More, Sir Walter Raleigh and more recently Rudolph Hess. Apart from its historic appeal, other major attractions of the Tower include the ravens, beefeaters and, of course, the Crown Jewels.

Tower Bridge was built to harmonise with the medieval appearance of the Tower and was opened in 1894. The central section was built so that it could be raised in order that ships could continue further upstream. The bridge now houses an exhibition and from the high-level walkways that link the two towers there are magnificent views over London.

Go under the road on the north side of Tower Bridge **A**, turn left and then immediately right to enter the St Katharine Docks. These former docks were built by Telford and opened in 1828. Since their closure in 1968, they have been redeveloped into an attractive marina lined by offices, flats, shops, restaurants, pubs and cafés. In one corner a Japanese-style garden has been created.

The area is well worth exploring thoroughly but the route keeps along the south side, and you should aim for the ship, the deep-sea trawler *Hatherlea*, berthed in West Dock. Continue between flats and office blocks, bearing right along St Katharine's Way, and at a Thames Path sign, turn first right and then left by the river. Turn left to rejoin the road and turn right along Wapping High Street, which is a fascinating mixture of open spaces, new houses,

St Katharine Docks – originally constructed by Thomas Telford between 1824 and 1828

renovated wharves, a few Victorian warehouses and luxury flats.

At regular intervals on the rest of the walk, Thames Walk waymarks direct you to the right for short sections beside the river, sometimes passing through metal gates, before returning to the road. You can either make these short forays to the riverside for the views across the Thames or ignore the footpath signs and continue along the road.

The route passes two old pubs, the Town of Ramsgate and the Captain Kidd, before turning left along New Crane Place. At the next Thames Path sign, turn right along Wapping Wall **B**, passing the Prospect of Whitby, which claims to be London's oldest waterside pub. Cross a bridge over Shadwell Basin and immediately turn right on to a

riverside path **C**. Pass along the right edge of the pleasant King Edward VII Memorial Park, which occupies the site of the old Shadwell fish market, and continue alongside the river – there is a fine view of Canary Wharf ahead – before turning left for the last time away from the Thames and around a right-hand bend on to a road **D**.

This is Narrow Street Limehouse, and you keep along it, passing several more old pubs (Barley Mow and the Grapes). Cross Limehouse Basin, where the Regent's Canal enters the Thames, and keep along the right edge of Ropemakers' Fields, a strip of parkland on the site where ropes for ships and mining used to be made. Continue as far as Three Colt Street, where a brief detour to the left leads to the impressive St Anne's Church, built by Hawksmoor and completed in 1724. Its tower is a major East End landmark.

The route continues to the right **E** along Three Colt Street. Turn left by the Enterprise pub, turn right, at a Thames Path sign, to a main road and turn left to traffic lights. Cross over, turn right in the Canary Wharf direction and, on the corner of Ontario Way, ascend the spiral staircase in the building opposite. Continue under an arcade to Westferry Circus, follow the curve of the circus to the left to cross West India Avenue and keep ahead to Canary Wharf Pier for one more view across the Thames. The Canary Wharf complex, one of the biggest recent building developments in Europe, is dominated by the tallest tower in the country, 800ft (243m) high and with a pyramid-shaped top. It can be seen from many of the other walks in this guide.

Return to West India Avenue, turn right and at a T-junction, keep ahead up steps and walk across Cabot Square. Ahead is Cabot Place and the Docklands Light Rail Canary Wharf Station. ●

Along the South Bank of the River Thames

Start	Westminster Bridge
Finish	London Bridge
Distance	3 miles (4.8km)
Approximate time	1½ hours
Refreshments	Pubs and cafés at Westminster and by London Bridge, some riverside pubs *en route*
Public transport	Underground to Westminster (District, Circle and Northern lines), return from London Bridge (Northern line)
Ordnance Survey maps	Landranger 176 (West London), Explorer 173 (London North, Harrow & Enfield)

After an initial opening stretch along the north bank of the river to Lambeth Bridge, the remainder of the walk follows the Thames Path along the south bank from Lambeth to London Bridge. There are striking views across the river to the Houses of Parliament, Somerset House and the dome of St Paul's, and the route passes the South Bank complex of arts buildings, the recently rebuilt Globe Theatre, Clink Prison Museum, Southwark Cathedral and the London Dungeon.

Begin on the north side of Westminster Bridge and walk along St Margaret Street, between the Houses of Parliament on the left and the church of St Margaret's Westminster and Westminster Abbey on the right. (For details of both the Houses of Parliament and Westminster Abbey, see Walk 5). Although inevitably overshadowed by the abbey, St Margaret's is a fine church in its own right. Built between 1486 and 1521, it has been the parish church of the House of Commons since 1614.

Just beyond Westminster Abbey is the 14th-century Jewel Tower, built by Edward III to store the royal treasures and one of the few parts of the medieval Palace of Westminster to survive. After passing the Victoria Tower of the Houses of Parliament, turn left, at a Thames Path sign, and take the path across Victoria Tower Gardens to the river. Turn right along the tree-lined embankment and go up steps to Lambeth Bridge Ⓐ. Turn left over the bridge and ahead is the church of St Mary-at-Lambeth, now the Museum of Garden History, and Lambeth Palace, the London residence of the archbishops of Canterbury.

On the other side, turn left down steps Ⓑ and continue along the embankment on the south side of the Thames back to Westminster Bridge. On this stretch of the walk, the views across the river to the Houses of Parliament

SCALE 1:25 000 or 2½ INCHES to 1 MILE 4CM to 1KM

| 0 | 200 | 400 | 600 | 800 METRES | 1 |
| 0 | 200 | 400 | 600 YARDS | ½ | KILOMETRES MILES |

are outstanding. After passing under Westminster Bridge, the route continues in front of County Hall – formerly the headquarters of the Greater London Council and now housing a hotel and the London Aquarium – and under Hungerford Bridge to the South Bank Arts Complex. This comprises the Royal Festival Hall (the only permanent legacy of the 1951 Festival of Britain), Queen Elizabeth Hall, National Film Theatre, Royal National Theatre and the Museum of the Moving Image. The latter is devoted to the history of film and television.

As you proceed, the long 18th-century façade of Somerset House is seen on the opposite bank, and soon the dome of St Paul's comes into view. After passing under the road and railway bridges at Blackfriars, the route continues through Bankside, once a notorious area for brothels and alehouses. Pass the disused Bankside Power Station, due to take on a new role as an extension of the Tate Gallery, and a little further on is the reconstructed Globe Theatre, opened in 1997 near the site of the original

the 14th-century great hall with a notable rose-window in the west gable. This was the London residence of the powerful bishops of Winchester, and occupied by them until 1649.

Turn right in front of the Golden Hinde Museum Ship at Pickford's Wharf – a replica of the ship in which Drake circumnavigated the world between 1577 and 1580 – to Southwark Cathedral **C**. This fine Gothic church, formerly the collegiate church of St Mary Overie, was elevated to cathedral status in 1905. The nave is a Victorian reconstruction – the original one fell into ruin – but the choir dates from the 13th century and is one of the earliest examples of Gothic architecture in London. Edmund Shakespeare, younger brother of the playwright, was buried here, and the memorial to his more famous brother is a reminder of the proximity of the Globe Theatre. The Harvard Chapel commemorates John Harvard, founder of the famous American university, who was baptised in the church.

Turn left and then right to pass along the north side of the cathedral, go under a bridge and keep ahead along Tooley Street to the London Dungeon. This is housed under some of the arches of London Bridge Station and is definitely not for the squeamish as it is devoted to methods of torture, execution and the more gruesome side of London's past.

Turn sharp right **D** up Duke Street Hill to the south side of London Bridge and, although the walk ends here, a short detour to the left along Borough High Street leads to the George, London's last remaining galleried inn. Apart from the cathedral, this ancient and much altered hostelry is the only building to survive from the days when Southwark was a centre of literature and drama, frequented by Shakespeare and other Elizabethan writers.

Elizabethan theatre associated with William Shakespeare.

Continue under Southwark Bridge, pass the attractive old Anchor Inn, built in 1755, turn right by the inn and turn left under a railway bridge into narrow Clink Street, lined by tall Victorian warehouses, which give it a dark and gloomy appearance and an appealing Dickensian atmosphere. The street is named after the notorious Clink Prison, from where the phrase 'in the clink' originated, which was nearby. One of the warehouses is now the Clink Prison Museum. There is also a remnant of Winchester Palace, mainly one wall of

West End – St James, Mayfair and Piccadilly

Start	Trafalgar Square
Distance	3½ miles (5.6km)
Approximate time	2 hours
Refreshments	Plenty of pubs, cafés and restaurants, especially around Shepherd Market and Piccadilly Circus
Public transport	Underground to Charing Cross (Bakerloo, Jubilee and Northern lines)
Ordnance Survey maps	Landranger 176 (West London), Explorer 173 (London North, Harrow & Enfield)

This walk leads through some of the most stylish and elegant parts of London's West End. Starting from Trafalgar Square, it takes in stretches of the Mall, Park Lane and Regent Street and includes the fashionable St James's, Berkeley, Grosvenor and Hanover squares. The route also passes the Ritz Hotel and the secluded and highly attractive enclave of Shepherd Market.

Trafalgar Square, named after Nelson's great victory over the French in 1805 and laid out in 1820, is inevitably dominated by the column erected in honour of the victor. The north side of the square is lined by the elegant Classical façade of the National Gallery, and in the north-east corner is the early-18th-century church of St Martin-in-the-Fields.

Start by going under Admiralty Arch in the south-west corner of the square and walk along the Mall, passing in front of the magnificent Carlton House Terrace, built by Nash in the early 19th century. Turn right up the steps that divide the two blocks of the terrace Ⓐ to the monument to the 'grand old Duke of York', keep ahead through Waterloo Place and turn left into Pall Mall.

Turn right into St James's Square, laid out by Henry Jermyn, Earl of

St Albans. In earlier centuries some of its grand houses were occupied by prime ministers and royal mistresses; in the gardens is a statue of William III. Walk along its east side, turn left and then turn right along Duke of York Street to St James's Church, Piccadilly, one of the few Wren churches outside the City Ⓑ. Turn left along Jermyn Street, at the end of the street turn right up to Piccadilly and turn left, passing the exclusive Ritz Hotel.

Turn right along Berkeley Street into Berkeley Square Ⓒ, made famous by both a film and a popular Second World War song. It was laid out in the 1730s and still retains some of its original houses on the west side. Turn left into the elegant and dignified Charles Street, turn left down Queen Street to Curzon Street and keep ahead under an arch into Shepherd Market Ⓓ. This secluded

SCALE 1:25000 or 2½ INCHES to 1 MILE 4CM to 1KM

0	200	400	600	800 METRES	1	
						KILOMETRES
						MILES
0	200	400	600 YARDS		½	

and attractive little enclave of narrow streets, lined with coffee shops, wine bars, restaurants and pubs, has an almost village-like atmosphere.

Return to Curzon Street, turn left to Park Lane and turn right along it. Hyde Park is over to the left. Turn right along Aldford Street ⓔ to the Grosvenor Chapel and turn left along South Audley Street into Grosvenor Square ⓕ. There is much American influence here. The US Embassy occupies the west side of the square, and there is a statue of President Franklin D. Roosevelt, paid for by the British people, in the gardens.

Turn right along Grosvenor Street, turn left into fashionable New Bond Street and turn right along Brook Street into Hanover Square, which has pleasant gardens and a statue to William Pitt the Younger. Keep ahead along Hanover Street to Regent Street and turn right ⓖ along it into Piccadilly Circus. Now one of London's principal shopping thoroughfares, Regent Street was laid out by Nash in the early 19th century, the backbone of his grand design that was to link the Prince Regent's Carlton House with his new development in Regent's Park. Bustling and garish Piccadilly Circus was originally just a road junction; later it became known as 'the hub of the Empire'.

Continue through Piccadilly Circus, turn right into the Haymarket and turn left along Cockspur Street to return to Trafalgar Square. ●

Berkeley Square – first laid out between 1739 and 1747

WEST END – ST JAMES, MAYFAIR AND PICCADILLY ● 21

Through the City of London

Start	Monument
Distance	3½ miles (5.6km)
Approximate time	2 hours
Refreshments	Plenty of pubs, restaurants and cafés
Public transport	Underground to Monument (Circle and District lines)
Ordnance Survey maps	Landranger 176 (West London), Explorer 173 (London North, Harrow & Enfield)

There is very much a Wren theme to this walk. It starts appropriately by the Monument to the Great Fire of London, the disaster that gave Wren his great opportunity, and includes St Paul's Cathedral, the greatest example of his architectural genius, plus a number of his other City churches. The route also passes some of the medieval churches that managed to survive the fire and takes in monuments to the City's legal and financial roles, as well as some of its administrative buildings. In addition there is a stretch along the north bank of the Thames.

The Monument was erected to commemorate the Great Fire of London which started in a bakery in nearby Pudding Lane on 2 September 1666 and destroyed thousands of houses, St Paul's Cathedral and 89 other churches, and many civic buildings. Sir Christopher Wren designed the Monument as well as rebuilding or restoring 51 of the City churches, most of them between 1670 and 1690. Some of these were destroyed by fire a second time as a result of enemy bombing in the Second World War and had to be restored again. The route passes many of these Wren churches, plus several others.

Begin by walking eastwards along Eastcheap as far as the church of St Margaret Pattens, the first of the series of Wren churches. Retrace your steps for a few yards and turn left down Lovat Lane, passing St Mary-at-Hill. At the bottom, turn right along Lower

Thames Street **Ⓐ**, passing the church of St Magnus the Martyr, continue along Upper Thames Street and turn left down Swan Lane to the river. From here the view embraces London Bridge and Tower Bridge to the left and the tower of Southwark Cathedral ahead.

Turn right along the Thames Path – this part is the Waterman's Walk – turn right again into All Hallows Lane, turn left along Steelyard Passage and at Cousin Lane, turn right back to Upper Thames Street **Ⓑ**. Turn left – on the right is St Michael, Paternoster Royal – and turn left along Broken Wharf back to the river.

The Thames Path is now called Paul's Walk. Pass under both the railway and road bridges at Blackfriars and shortly afterwards climb steps to the road. As you continue along the Victoria Embankment, the greenery seen over to the right is the Temple Gardens. At a sign 'Middle Temple, Inner Temple, Temple Church', turn right through a gate into the gardens 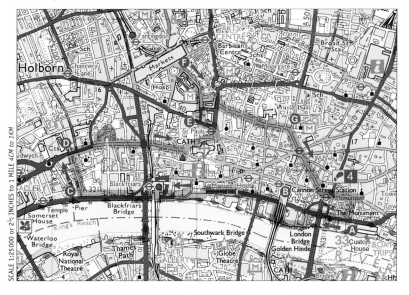. This area of small squares and Georgian buildings contains two of the Inns of Court – Middle Temple and Inner Temple – and is a haven of tranquillity amidst the bustle of the city. Many leading lawyers have their chambers here. Keep ahead under an arch and turn right through Pump Court to the Temple Church, a fine, 12th-century round church that belonged to the Crusading Order of Knights Templars – hence the name Temple. There are some superb effigies of some of the medieval knights.

Turn left in front of the church and go under an arch into Fleet Street. Turn right, pass St Dunstan-in-the-West and at a sign to Dr Johnson's House, turn left through Johnson's Court and follow the signposted route round a series of bends to emerge into Gough Square, another peaceful City enclave. Dr Johnson compiled his dictionary while living at No. 17, an elegant early-18th-century house, from 1748 to 1759.

Turn right to walk through the square, go under an arch into Gunpowder Square and turn right along Wine Office Court, passing Ye Olde Cheshire Cheese, an atmospheric old City tavern where Johnson and his circle – Boswell, Garrick, Gibbon, Reynolds and others – used to meet. Among its later patrons were Carlyle, Tennyson and Dickens.

After returning to Fleet Street, turn left, passing St Bride's on the right, well worth a visit. The almost complete destruction of this Wren church in 1940 revealed archaeological evidence – now on display in the crypt – of the earlier Roman origins of the site. Continue to Ludgate Circus and keep ahead up Ludgate Hill to St Paul's Cathedral, passing St Martin-within-Ludgate.

Wren was appropriately the first person to be buried in St Paul's, and the inscription on his tomb – situated in the crypt near those of Nelson and Wellington – reads: *Si monumentum requiris, Circumspice* (If you need a monument, look around you). There could certainly be no finer monument to his genius than this magnificent and spacious church, started in 1675 and completed in 1709 on the site of the

Dr Johnson's House in Gough Square

vast medieval cathedral destroyed by the Great Fire. It is England's only major Classical cathedral, and the great dome, still a major London landmark despite being overshadowed by modern office blocks, is an outstanding architectural composition and ranks with that of St Peter's in Rome.

Keep to the left of the cathedral through St Paul's Churchyard, turn left to Newgate Street, turn left again and turn right by the ruined Christ Church Greyfriars into King Edward Street **E**. Continue along the street called Little Britain, which bends left, between the buildings of St Bartholomew's Hospital, to emerge into West Smithfield in front of Smithfield Market **F**. The half-timbered gateway on the right leads to the delightful church of St Bartholomew-the-Great, founded as a priory in 1123 and the oldest parish church in London. The nave was demolished during the dissolution of the monasteries but the chancel has survived centuries of neglect and retains some of its early-Norman arches.

Retrace your steps along Little Britain and turn left through the attractive garden of Postman's Park, opened in

1880 and created from several adjacent churchyards. Pass the late-18th-century church of St Botolph-without-Aldersgate to emerge into Aldersgate Street, turn right and take the first turning on the left, Gresham Street. Pass the brick church of St Anne and St Agnes and continue to the church of St Lawrence Jewry. This fine Wren church, so called because its medieval predecessor was located within the Jewish quarter of the City, is now the church of the Corporation of London. The Guildhall, the administrative headquarters of the City since the 12th century, is to the left. Although considerably restored over the centuries, especially following the great fires of 1666 and 1940, the buildings date back mainly to the early 15th century. The Great Hall, scene of many historic occasions – including the trials of Lady Jane Grey and Archbishop Cranmer – is one of the finest surviving medieval structures in London.

Continue along Gresham Street and turn right into Princes Street **G** to a junction of several roads. Around this junction and in close proximity is the 18th-century Mansion House, official residence of the Lord Mayor of London, and three of the major institutions of the City. These are the Bank of England, founded in 1694 and rebuilt in the early 19th century and again in 1924, the modern Stock Exchange and Royal Exchange. The latter was founded in 1566 as a meeting-place for merchants but the present building is Victorian.

Keep ahead towards the Monument – clearly visible – passing the early-18th-century church of St Edmund the King and Martyr, and St Mary Woolnoth, which is a rare example of a City church not built by Wren. It was the work of his pupil Nicholas Hawksmoor. Finally, you pass St Clement's before arriving back at the start. ●

Royal parks and palaces of Central London

Start	Parliament Square
Finish	Kensington High Street
Distance	4 miles (6.4km)
Approximate time	2 hours
Refreshments	Pubs, restaurants and cafés at Westminster and Kensington, kiosks and cafés in St James's Park and Hyde Park
Public transport	Underground to Westminster (District, Circle and Northern lines), return from High Street Kensington (Circle and District lines)
Ordnance Survey maps	Landranger 176 (West London), Explorer 173 (London North, Harrow & Enfield)

The adjacent royal parks of St James's, the Green, Hyde and Kensington Gardens make up a huge green block in the very heart of the capital. This route links the four parks and the various royal palaces associated with them, enabling you to enjoy an almost entirely rural walk from the Palace of Westminster, better known as the Houses of Parliament, to Kensington Palace across continuous parkland and for the most part away from traffic. On the way you catch a glimpse of Buckingham Palace and pass by St James's Palace.

Parliament Square contains statues of several great national leaders, including one of Churchill in a typically belligerent wartime pose. He is facing the vast bulk of the Houses of Parliament, built in the middle of the 19th century to the designs of Sir Charles Barry and Augustus Pugin after most of its predecessor was destroyed by fire in 1834. The buildings stand on the site of the medieval royal palace of Westminster but little of this survived the fire apart from the late-11th-century Westminster Hall. The hall has been the setting for a number of famous trials, including those of Guy Fawkes in 1605

and Charles I in 1649. It is particularly noted for its magnificent 14th-century hammerbeam roof.

On the other side of the road stands Westminster Abbey. Since the original Saxon minster was rebuilt by Edward the Confessor shortly before the Norman Conquest, it has been the coronation place of English monarchs, and many are also buried here. The present church dates mainly from the 13th century, when it was extensively rebuilt again by Henry III. The Henry VII Chapel at the east end was added in the early 16th century, and the abbey was heavily restored by Wren and

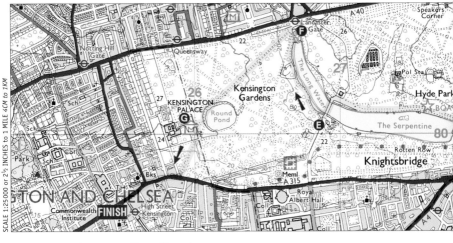

SCALE 1:25000 or 2½ INCHES to 1 MILE 4CM to 1KM

0	200	400	600	800 METRES	1
					KILOMETRES
					MILES
0	200	400	600 YARDS	½	

Hawksmoor in the early 18th century. Apart from the royal tombs, the interior contains a huge number of memorials to statesmen, writers, artists, soldiers, scientists and others, including the tomb of the Unknown Warrior. Plenty of time needs to be devoted to a visit to this vast repository of much of the nation's history.

Start from the north side of Parliament Square and walk along Parliament Street towards the Cenotaph. Turn left into King Great Charles Street, walking between the imposing govern-ment buildings of the Treasury to the left and the Foreign and Common-wealth Office to the right, and descend steps by the statue of Robert Clive (Clive of India). To the left is the entrance to the underground Cabinet War Rooms. This is where meetings of the Wartime Cabinet were held and where Churchill used to sleep through-out the Blitz.

Cross the road into St James's Park and turn right on to a path that curves left to keep beside the lake. To the right is a fine view across Horse Guards Parade. Walk beside the lake as far as a crossing of paths to the right of a bridge **A**. The views from the bridge – looking

towards Whitehall in one direction and the façade of Buckingham Palace in the other – are most impressive. Turn right at the crossroads to emerge on to the Mall, cross over and take the road opposite, passing between St James's Palace on the left and the Queen's Chapel on the right. The latter was completed in the early 17th century by Inigo Jones for Queen Henrietta Maria, wife of Charles I.

Turn left along Pall Mall **B** to pass in front of St James's Palace. This mainly Tudor structure, built by Henry VIII, was the principal royal residence until superseded by Buckingham Palace in the reign of George IV; foreign ambas-sadors are still accredited to the Court of St James's. At the end of Pall Mall, keep ahead along Cleveland Row – Clarence House is to the left – pass to the right of Selwyn House and keep ahead along a path into the Green Park. Turn left to pass by the early-19th-century Lancaster House, take the first turning on the right and, at a junction of three paths, turn sharply right to continue across the park. Bear right on joining another path and, before reaching Piccadilly, turn left **C** to continue along the right edge of the park to Hyde Park Corner.

Negotiate the busy crossing here via two subways **D**. First comes the Green

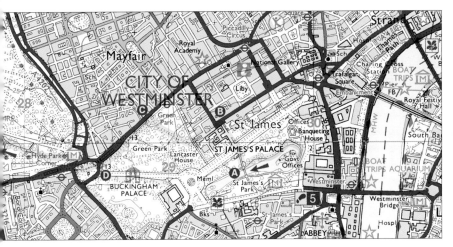

Park Subway and this is followed by a stretch of path that curves left, passing to the right of a statue of the Duke of Wellington. The 'Iron Duke' is appropriately overlooking Apsley House, a fine Georgian mansion that was his London residence. Then go under the Hyde Park Corner Subway, following signs to Hyde Park, and on emerging from it, turn left and left again to pass through the gates into the park.

Cross a road, turn left along a path that runs parallel to the sandy riding-track of Rotten Row on the left and turn half-right to enter the Rose Garden. Continue through it, keep ahead to a T-junction, turn right to a more complex junction and turn left to follow a drive along the right edge of the Serpentine. Turn left to cross a bridge over it and turn right into Kensington Gardens **E**.

At a junction, take the path to the right, signposted Peter Pan and Italian Fountain, which keeps close to the left bank of Long Water. Pass the well-known Peter Pan statue and continue to the delightful Italian Gardens on the right. Just before reaching the edge of the park, turn sharply left **F** on to a path that cuts across the park to an obelisk, erected in 1864 to Speke, the explorer. Continue past it, following signs to Kensington Palace, to the Round Pond, follow the edge of the pond as it curves left and take the first turning on the right to the Broad Walk **G**. In front is Kensington Palace and the statue of Queen Victoria, who was born in the palace in 1819 and first heard of her accession to the throne here 18 years later.

In 1689 William III and Mary II bought the modest Nottingham House that stood here and gave Wren the job of redesigning and enlarging it into the present Kensington Palace. For many years it was a principal royal residence and still has private apartments for members of the royal family. It was the home of Diana, Princess of Wales, and in the autumn of 1997 became the main focal point for the outpouring of public grief that followed her death.

Turn right if visiting the State Apartments and Orangery but the route continues to the left along the Broad Walk, laid out by Caroline of Anspach, wife of George II. Take the first path on the right, then turn left and walk diagonally across the park to emerge on to Kensington High Street. To the right is an imposing view of the main front of the palace and the statue of William III. Turn right along Kensington High Street to the Underground station. ●

Horsenden Hill

Start	Horsenden Hill car park, at top of Horsenden Lane
Distance	2½ miles (4km). Add ¾ mile (1.2km) if coming from Perivale Station and pick up the walk at point **Ⓓ**
Approximate time	1½ hours (2 hours from Perivale Station)
Parking	Horsenden Hill
Refreshments	Pub near start
Public transport	Underground to Perivale (Central line). Turn right to pass under the railway bridge, keep ahead and, on approaching a canal bridge, turn right down steps to the towpath to join the main walk at point **Ⓓ**
Ordnance Survey maps	Landranger 176 (West London), Explorer 173 (London North, Harrow & Enfield)

Horsenden Hill, which rises to 279ft (85m) above west London, plus the meadows below it stretching to the banks of the Grand Union Canal, together make up a rural and unspoilt oasis that has managed to survive amidst a predominantly suburban landscape. The terrain is an attractive combination of woodland and meadowland, with a pleasant stretch along the canal towpath, and there are fine and extensive views from the summit.

For the almost miraculous preservation of this small but intensely valuable area of countryside, we are indebted to

Middlesex County Council, who bought it as a public recreation area when surrounding suburban expansion was at its height in the 1930s. Now it is maintained by Ealing Borough Council.

The Grand Union Canal below Horsenden Hill

Start by walking back towards the road but, just before it, turn right on to a tarmac path that heads downhill, keeping parallel to the road (Horsenden Lane) and emerging on to it by the Ballot Box pub. Keep ahead in front of the pub and just beyond it turn right along a tree-lined tarmac path **A**. Follow it as far as a metal barrier, where you turn right to enter Horsenden Wood **B**.

Immediately take the left-hand path at a fork, cross a track and keep ahead, climbing gently all the while. Turn right on joining another path, continue uphill along the right edge of a golf-course and, when you see the triangulation pillar that marks the summit, turn left to head across to it **C**. The contrasting views from here are superb: looking eastwards across the mass of built-up London and westwards over the suburbs towards the more rural delights of the distant Chilterns.

Continue past the triangulation pillar, making for the right corner of the open grassy area on the top of Horsenden Hill, and take a path that leads down steps and winds through thick woodland to emerge from the trees. Keep along the right edge of rough grassland to reach a crossing of grassy paths, just after passing to the right of a solitary oak tree. Turn left downhill into trees again, pass beside a barrier on to a road and turn left to cross a footbridge over the Grand Union Canal.

If returning to Perivale Station, continue along the road.

Just after crossing the canal bridge, turn left **D** down steps to the towpath and turn left along it, passing under the bridge. Keep along the towpath – Perivale Wood is to the left – as far as a wooden footbridge. After passing under it, turn left **E** through a metal gate, at a public footpath sign, along a path that curves left uphill to a T-junction. Turn

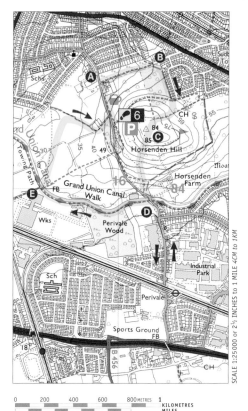

sharp left to cross the bridge – ahead is a fine view of Horsenden Hill – then turn first sharp right and then left to go through another metal kissing-gate. Turn left on to a path that keeps along the right edge of a playing-field, by a hedge and trees on the right, and in the field corner turn right through a gap in the line of trees.

Continue along the left edge of a meadow, pass through another gap, turn left by a hedge on the left and, in the corner of the meadow, keep ahead through trees to join a clear path. Turn right, head gently uphill along this hedge-lined path and, about 50 yds (46m) before reaching a barrier, turn right on to another path into woodland. Turn left at a fork, go up steps on to a road, continue up the steps on the opposite side and turn right on to a tarmac path to return to the start. ●

Parkland Walk from Finsbury Park to Highgate

Start	Finsbury Park Station
Finish	Highgate Station
Distance	3½ miles (5.6km). Shorter version 2 miles (3.2km)
Approximate time	2 hours (1 hour for shorter walk)
Refreshments	Pubs and cafés at Finsbury Park; pubs, cafés and restaurants at Highgate; café in Highgate Wood
Public transport	Underground to Finsbury Park (Piccadilly and Victoria lines), return from Highgate (Northern line)
Ordnance Survey maps	Landranger 176 (West London), Explorer 173 (London North, Harrow & Enfield)

From the initially unpromising surroundings of Finsbury Park Station, a disused railway track provides an attractive 'green corridor' through a heavily built-up area of north London. The shorter version finishes at Highgate but the full walk does a short circuit around the adjacent Queen's and Highgate woods, both beautiful remnants of the extensive ancient woodlands that once covered much of the old county of Middlesex.

Turn left in front of the station, cross Stroud Green Road and at a 'Welcome to Parkland Walk' notice, go through an entrance in a wall. A winding brick path leads to an enclosed, hedge-lined and curving path that continues alongside the main railway line on the left to a T-junction.

Turn left to cross a footbridge over the railway and turn right **A** to continue along the disused railway track, which used to connect Finsbury Park Station with Alexandra Palace. You keep along this attractive, tree-lined track for the next 1¼ miles (2.8km), sometimes running along the top of an embankment and sometimes through deep, wooded cuttings. At one point the route passes between former station platforms. Eventually you bear

left up to a road. Turn right along it to a T-junction and turn right again along the main road to a crossroads **B**.

For the short walk, keep ahead along Archway Road to Highgate Station.

If doing the complete walk that

On the Parkland Walk

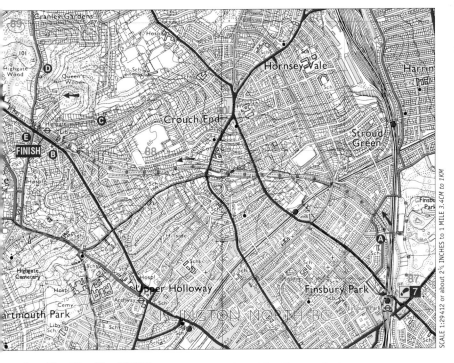

SCALE 1:29412 or about 2¼ INCHES to 1 MILE 3.4CM to 1KM

```
0   200   400   600   800 METRES  1
                                      KILOMETRES
0   200   400   600 YARDS   ½         MILES
```

involves a short circuit of Queen's
and Highgate woods, turn right into
Shepherd's Hill and, just before
Highgate Library, turn left through a
hedge gap on to a path that heads
gently downhill through trees. Descend
some steps, continue along an enclosed
path to a road, turn right and, where the
road curves right, turn left at a sign
'Footpath through Queen's Wood to
Wood Lane, Highgate, Muswell Hill
Road and Park Road Crouch End', on to
a tarmac path **C**. The path descends
into Queen's Wood, and in front of an
information board at the bottom of the
hill take the right-hand path, which
heads gently uphill through this beautiful area of ancient woodland to a road.

Cross over, continue along the path
opposite, immediately taking the left-
hand path at a fork, and turn left at a
T-junction. Turn right at a crossing of
paths and, ignoring all side turns,
continue through the wood, bearing

right and heading gently down to a
footpath sign. Bear left, in the Muswell
Hill Road direction, and head up to
another footpath sign at a T-junction.
Turn left along a track, in the Muswell
Hill Road and Highgate Wood direction,
and follow it to a road **D**.

Cross over to enter Highgate Wood,
a public area maintained by the
Corporation of the City of London since
1886. Take the path to the right and
bear right on joining another path. The
path gradually bears left through more
delightful woodland to a crossway
where, to the left, a building can be
seen. Turn left to this building – a café
and toilet block – and take the path to
the left of it to join a track. This track
initially keeps along the right, inside
edge of the woodland, later re-enters
the trees, passes to the left of a
children's play area and bears slightly
left to continue through the wood to
a metal gate. Go through, turn right
along a road **E** and at a junction turn
left along Archway Road to Highgate
Station.

Wimbledon Common

Start	Wimbledon Common Windmill, at end of Windmill Road
Distance	3½ miles (5.6km). Add 1½ miles (2.4km) if coming from Wimbledon Station and pick up the walk at point **Ⓑ**
Approximate time	1½ hours (2½ hours from Wimbledon Station)
Parking	Car park by Wimbledon Common Windmill
Refreshments	Pubs and cafés in Wimbledon village, tearoom at Wimbledon Common Windmill
Public transport	Trains from London (Waterloo) or Underground to Wimbledon (District line). Turn right, head up Wimbledon Hill Road to a T-junction and turn right along High Street through Wimbledon village. Turn left at the next T-junction, continue along Parkside to the common and at a fork by a war memorial take the left-hand road. After crossing a road you join the main walk
Ordnance Survey maps	Landranger 176 (West London), Explorer 161 (London South, Croydon & Esher)

First-time visitors who expect smooth expanses of grassy parkland are in for something of a shock for much of Wimbledon Common, and the adjacent Putney Heath to the north, comprise rough heathland and thick woodland – a genuinely rural oasis amidst suburban south London. The walk does a circuit of the common and passes by the remains of a prehistoric fort and several ponds. There are plenty of refreshment facilities in nearby Wimbledon village, easily reached from point **Ⓑ**.

In the past Wimbledon Common seems to have been a favourite venue for duelling; the last one occurred in 1840. It extends over 1000 acres (405ha) and has been protected by an Act of Parliament since 1871. Wimbledon Common Windmill was erected in 1817 on the site of an earlier one. A plaque states that Lord Baden-Powell wrote part of his *Scouting for Boys* while living here.

From the Windmill, walk back along the road to a junction, turn right and pass beside a metal barrier. Keep ahead

along a straight track, take the first path on the left **Ⓐ** and follow it across the common, initially along the right edge of open grassland and later between trees, to a road.

Walkers returning to Wimbledon Station should cross over and continue along the track ahead to the war memorial, where they pick up the outward route and retrace their steps to the station.

Turn right on to a path alongside the road and, where a riding-track crosses the road about 100 yds (91m) before

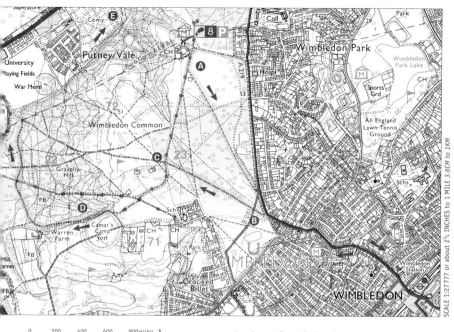

SCALE 1:27777 or about 2¼ INCHES to 1 MILE 3.6CM to 1KM

0 200 400 600 800 METRES 1
                                KILOMETRES
                                MILES
0 200 400 600 YARDS   ½

reaching the Causeway, turn sharp right **B** on to a path that keeps parallel to this riding-track on the right. Cross a road and keep ahead through trees and across rough grassland – ignoring all side turns – until the path emerges into a more open area at a major crossing of paths and tracks **C**. Turn left along a broad track, which curves right across part of the Royal Wimbledon Golf Course, to a fork and continue along the left-hand track to reach a tarmac drive.

Cross over, walk along the track opposite towards trees and, on entering them, bear left to continue through this delightful woodland. The tree-covered low mound on the left is all that remains of Caesar's Camp which, despite its name, is a prehistoric fort. It was badly damaged by a Victorian owner of the site.

Look out for a fork, where you take the right-hand track **D** – passing between three upright concrete posts – which heads gently downhill, initially keeping parallel to the other track but then curving right. Keep on the main track all the while, which later curves right again to continue along the left, inside edge of the common. The buildings of Putney Vale can be seen to the left, and later the track keeps along the right edge of a cemetery.

Where a path leads off to the right over a brick culvert in a ditch **E** – it leaves the track opposite a gate into the cemetery – follow it to the attractive and secluded Queen's Mere. On the left side of the pool, turn left, at a post waymarked with a fish and arrow, on to an uphill path through woodland. Bear right, following the regular waymarked posts, and the path emerges on to open grassland by the windmill.

Wimbledon Common

Osterley Park and the Grand Union Canal

Start	Osterley Park
Distance	4½ miles (7.2km). Add 1 mile (1.6km) if coming from Osterley Station and pick up the walk at point **Ⓐ**
Approximate time	2½ hours (3 hours from Osterley Station)
Parking	Osterley Park
Refreshments	Pub at Wyke Green; pub and café at Norwood Green, tearoom at Osterley Park
Public transport	Underground to Osterley (Piccadilly line). Turn left, take the first turning on the left and at a T-junction keep ahead through the gates of the park. Walk along the main drive and look out for a metal kissing-gate on the right, where you join the main walk at point **Ⓐ**
Ordnance Survey maps	Landranger 176 (West London), Explorer 161 (London South, Croydon & Esher)

This is a varied walk that leads from the expanses of Osterley Park to the towpath of the Grand Union Canal and on through part of the Brent River Park to Norwood Green. Historic interest ranges from Osterley Park House to Brunel's Three Bridges at Hanwell, which are a marvel of the Industrial Revolution.

From the car park, walk back along the broad, tree-lined drive and look out for a metal kissing-gate on the left **Ⓐ**. Go through it, walk along a path enclosed between wire fences and follow it around first a right and then a left bend. Where the path peters out, keep ahead along the left edge of a green, cross a track and continue to a road opposite the Hare and Hounds at Wyke Green.

Turn left along the road – busy but quite pleasant – pass under the M4 motorway and after about ½ mile (800m), turn right beside a barrier on to a track **Ⓑ** and immediately bear left to a kissing-gate. Go through, walk along a narrow enclosed path, by a high wire fence bordering a sports ground on the left, and at the corner of this fence, keep

ahead through a metal gate and bear right to cross a railway line. Keep ahead to a road, continue along it and, after crossing a canal bridge, turn right down steps to the towpath **Ⓒ**. Turn sharp right to pass under the bridge and continue along the towpath of the Grand Union Canal for the next 1¼ miles (2km), passing by the Hanwell Flight of Locks.

This stretch forms part of the Brent River Park, an important area for nature and landscape conservation in west London, which extends along about 4½ miles (7.2km) of the River Brent and canal. After nearly 1 mile (1.6km), you reach Three Bridges, where the canal both crosses the railway and goes under the road. This intersection was designed by Brunel in 1855–6 and is unique in

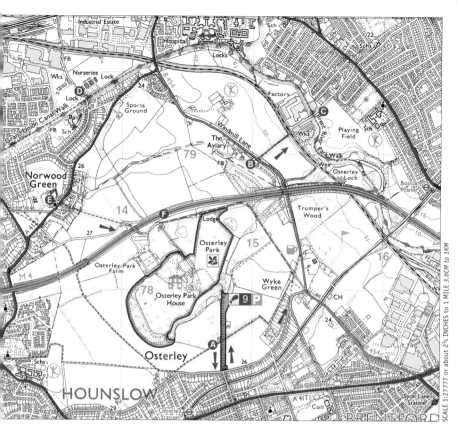

SCALE 1:27777 or about 2¼ INCHES to 1 MILE 3.6CM to 1KM

0	200	400	600	800 METRES	1
					KILOMETRES
					MILES
0	200	400	600 YARDS	½	

the way that three different modes of transport cross in one place.

After passing under the next bridge – No. 204 and painted white – go up steps **D**, turn right and right again to cross the bridge and keep ahead to a road, Melbury Avenue. Walk along it to a T-junction, turn left and, at the next T-junction, turn right along Tentelow Lane into Norwood Green. Turn left at the side of the Plough, at a public footpath sign 'Footpath Leading to St Mary's Avenue' **E**, walk along an enclosed path, cross a road and take the enclosed path opposite.

The path continues in a straight line across the middle of a large field, and on the far side climb steps on to a lane and keep ahead to cross a bridge over the M4. The lane curves left. In front of

gates turn right on to a tarmac track **F** and go through a gate to re-enter Osterley Park. Keep ahead along the straight, tree-lined track – later passing under an attractive avenue of trees – and bear right to go through a metal gate. The track passes in front of the house and curves left to keep alongside the Garden Lake on the right.

The redbrick Osterley Park House was originally an Elizabethan mansion built for Thomas Gresham, the founder of the Royal Exchange in the City of London. Its present appearance is the result of a complete transformation by Robert Adam in 1761. Inside there is a superb collection of Adam furniture and fittings. In 1949 the house and its parkland were given to the National Trust.

Follow the track to the right around the end of the Garden Lake and, at a sign, turn left along a short stretch of path to return to the car park. ●

Chelsea and Battersea Park

Start	Chelsea, Sloane Square
Distance	4 miles (6.4km)
Approximate time	2 hours
Refreshments	Pubs, cafés and restaurants at Chelsea; café in Battersea Park
Public transport	Underground to Sloane Square (Circle and District lines)
Ordnance Survey maps	Landranger 176 (West London), Pathfinder 1175, TQ 27/37 (Wimbledon & Dulwich)

From busy Sloane Square, a walk through the grounds and parkland surrounding the Royal Hospital at Chelsea leads down to the Thames and the Chelsea Embankment. Then follows an exploration of the delightful area around Cheyne Walk, before crossing Albert Bridge for a tour of part of Battersea Park on the south side of the river. You recross the Thames via Chelsea Bridge to return to the start.

Start by walking through Sloane Square and on along King's Road. Turn left into Cheltenham Terrace **A**, passing the early-19th-century Duke of York's Headquarters on the left, continue along Franklin's Row and at a T-junction by the Royal Hospital, keep ahead through London Gate into the hospital grounds.

The Royal Hospital at Chelsea, designed by Wren, was founded in 1682 by Charles II as a retirement home for old and disabled soldiers. Today it houses over 400 'Chelsea Pensioners', resplendent in their distinctive scarlet coats and three-cornered hats. Pass beside Garden Gate, keep ahead along a broad, tree-lined drive and take the first path on the right **B** to continue in front of the south – the most impressive – façade of the hospital. In front of the gates, turn left along a gravel path and go through gates on to the Chelsea Embankment **C**. Turn right beside the

river towards Albert Bridge and, at traffic lights, turn right and then immediately left to continue along Cheyne Walk, lined with trees and dignified 18th-century houses.

Briefly rejoin the Embankment by Albert Bridge but then keep ahead along another section of Cheyne Walk. At the King's Head and Eight Bells pub, turn right along Cheyne Row, another delightful street of handsome and

Cheyne Walk, Chelsea

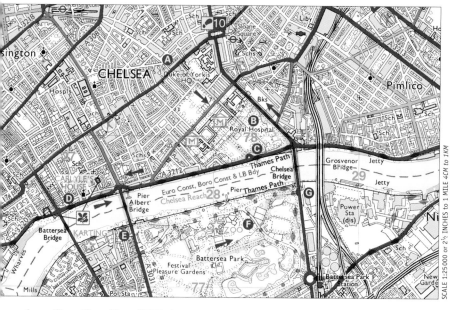

SCALE 1:25000 or 2½ INCHES to 1 MILE 4CM to 1KM

| 0 | 200 | 400 | 600 | 800 METRES | 1 |
| 0 | 200 | 400 | 600 YARDS | ½ | KILOMETRES MILES |

elegant houses. This area of Chelsea has always attracted writers and artists, and among those who have lived here are James McNeil Whistler, J.M. Turner, Bram Stoker, Hilaire Belloc, George Eliot, Thomas Carlyle and more recently Mick Jagger. Carlyle's house – No. 24 – is now owned by the National Trust.

Turn left into Upper Cheyne Row, left again into Lawrence Street, turn right along Justice Walk and turn left along Old Church Street to Chelsea Old Church **D**. This ancient church, founded in the 12th century, was badly damaged in an air raid in 1941 and had to be almost rebuilt. It is particularly associated with Sir Thomas More who worshipped here; his statue is outside.

Continue to the left along the Embankment again to Albert Bridge and turn right over it. At a Riverside Walk sign, turn left through a gate into Battersea Park **E**. Walk initially beside the Thames and take the first tarmac path on the right. Turn left at a T-junction a few yards ahead and, about 50 yds (46m) after joining a

broad drive, turn right down steps, and ahead is an attractive view over the park, created in 1853 from former marshland. Make for a small rectangular pool, pass along its right side, go up steps and keep ahead, bearing slightly right, to a T-junction.

Turn left to the next junction of paths and turn left again along a broad, tree-lined drive, passing a bandstand and continuing to the edge of a boating-lake. To the right is a 19th-century pump house, now a gallery and information centre for the park. Walk alongside the lake, go through a gate on to a broad drive, turn left and take the first path on the right **F**. The path, passing between tennis-courts on the left and a running-track on the right, bears gradually right to a drive.

Turn right along the drive to emerge from the park in front of Battersea Power Station, built in 1934 and now redundant. Turn left **G** to recross the Thames by Chelsea Bridge, keep ahead along Chelsea Bridge Road – on the left are the grounds of the Royal Hospital and on the right are army barracks – and continue along Lower Sloane Street to return to Sloane Square. ●

Along the Thames from Richmond to Kew

Start	Richmond Station
Finish	Kew Gardens Station
Distance	5 miles (8km)
Approximate time	2½ hours
Parking	Richmond Station
Refreshments	Pubs, cafés and restaurants at Richmond; riverside pubs at Strand on the Green; pubs and cafés at Kew
Public transport	Trains from London (Waterloo) or Underground to Richmond (District line), return by Underground from Kew Gardens (District line)
Ordnance Survey maps	Landranger 176 (West London), Explorer 161 (London South, Croydon & Esher)

The route follows a pleasant and mainly tree-lined stretch of the River Thames from Twickenham Bridge at Richmond to Kew Bridge. There are fine views across the river, and at both ends of the walk you pass outstanding examples of period houses: around Richmond Green near the start and at Strand on the Green and Kew Green near the finish. In addition there are three fine riverside pubs at Strand on the Green. There is also the opportunity to visit the world-famous Royal Botanic Gardens at Kew.

With its rural surroundings, splendid riverside location and proximity to the extensive park, Richmond has always been one of the most desirable areas near London. The area used to be known as Shene but after Henry VII built a new palace here in the late 15th century he renamed it Richmond after his earldom in Yorkshire.

Turn left out of the station and at traffic lights turn right along Duke Street **Ⓐ** into the elegant and spacious Richmond Green, one of the largest in the country and lined by a mixture of houses, including some splendid Queen Anne and early-Georgian residences. Turn half-left on to a path that runs diagonally across the green and at a crossing of paths about half-way across, bear left, and the path brings you out opposite Old Palace Yard. The arch in front and some of the brickwork in the adjoining houses is all that remains of the huge palace built by Henry VII, founder of the Tudor dynasty. He died there in 1509, as did the last of the Tudors, Elizabeth I, in 1603. It was neglected and partially demolished during the Cromwellian period and subsequently abandoned by later Stuart monarchs.

After passing under the arch, bear right along the edge of a green and turn right along an enclosed path to a road.

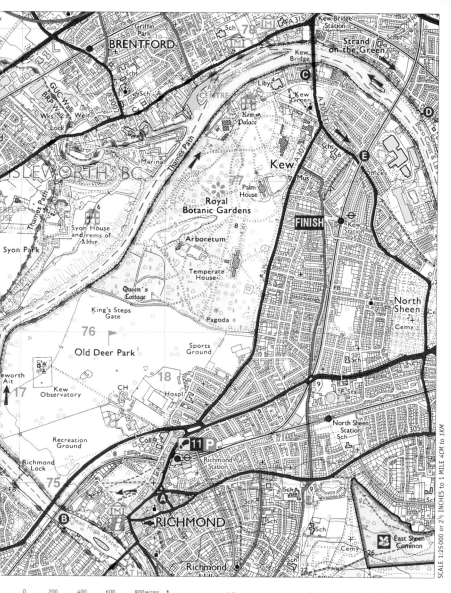

SCALE 1:25000 or 2½ INCHES to 1 MILE 4CM to 1KM

0	200	400	600	800 METRES	1
					KILOMETRES
					MILES
0	200	400	600 YARDS	½	

Turn left to the Thames and turn right on to a riverside path, signposted to Richmond Gardens, Kew Gardens and Kew Bridge **Ⓑ**.

Pass under first a railway bridge, then Twickenham Bridge and third a footbridge by Richmond Lock. The next bridge, Kew Bridge, is nearly 2½ miles (4km) miles further on. As you proceed towards it along the Thames Path, the wide-open spaces of the Old Deer Park on the right give way later to Kew Gardens and, towards the end, comes a view of the 17th-century Kew Palace which, despite its modest size, was a favourite residence of George III and his family. The palace is in the grounds of the Royal Botanic Gardens, Kew. These internationally renowned gardens, first started in the 17th century and subsequently extended, are accessible either from the riverside path or from Kew Green near the end of the walk.

They require and merit a lengthy visit.

To the left across the river the views are first of Isleworth church and later of Syon Park and House, the latter a remodelled Tudor mansion owned by the dukes of Northumberland. Eventually, Kew Bridge comes into sight. In front of the bridge **⊙** turn right down steps, walk along a track and turn sharp left up steps to a road for a short detour to Strand on the Green. Cross the bridge, turn left down steps towards the river again and turn left along the Thames Path (North Side), in the Chiswick Bridge direction. Pass under the bridge, turn left along a path and turn sharp right along a road. The road curves left and, at a footpath sign to Strand on the Green, bear right to continue along a riverside path, passing in front of the delightful collection of houses and cottages that make up Strand on the Green, once a small fishing hamlet on the Thames. There are three appealing pubs here: Bell and Crown, City Barge and Bull's Head. The latter is just beyond the railway bridge, and from here **⊙** you retrace your steps back over Kew Bridge to rejoin the Thames Path (South Side) **⊙**.

Pass under the bridge again and after about 200 yds (183m) turn right down steps and walk along a paved path, passing in front of cottages and along the left edge of a small recreation ground. Turn left along a tarmac drive and turn right to emerge on to Kew Green which, despite the traffic, has managed to retain something of a village atmosphere. It is lined by some fine old houses, cricket is still played here, and there are two pubs, a duck pond and a small, early-18th-century church.

Keep ahead, passing to the right of the duck pond, bear left along the main road and turn down the first road on the left (Mortlake Road). Take the second turning on the right into Leyborne Park **⊙**, immediately bear right along an enclosed path to a road and turn left to Kew Gardens Station. ●

Richmond Green

Hampstead Heath

Start	Hampstead Station
Distance	4½ miles (7.2km)
Approximate time	2 hours
Refreshments	Pubs, cafés and restaurants at Hampstead, three pubs on the heath; café and restaurant at Kenwood House
Public transport	Underground to Hampstead (Northern line)
Ordnance Survey maps	Landranger 176 (West London), Explorer 173 (London North, Harrow & Enfield)

The heathland, woodland and grassland of Hampstead Heath, a traditional and highly popular recreational area for Londoners, extends over 800 acres (324ha) of north London and, unlike the royal parks of Central London, is a substantial wedge of surprisingly authentic and untamed countryside close to the city. It is also quite hilly and from its higher points, especially the 320ft- (98m) high vantage point of Parliament Hill, there are superb and extensive views over London. Starting from Hampstead village, the walk does a circuit of the heath, passing three well-known pubs, and includes the elegant, 18th-century Kenwood House.

With narrow alleys and winding streets, small squares and picturesque cottages, Hampstead retains its village-like atmosphere more perhaps than any other area of London. In the 18th century it became a fashionable spa, and a number of handsome houses date from that period. Its almost rural, hilltop position on the edge of the heath – out of the city but not too far away – has long made Hampstead a desirable place to live.

Turn right out of the station, walk up Heath Street to the edge of the heath and keep ahead towards Jack Straw's Castle, an 18th-century inn, though almost totally rebuilt in the 1960s. It is named after one of the leaders of the Peasants' Revolt, who is alleged to have gathered together a mob near here in

1381. Just after passing Whitestone Pond on the left – and before reaching the inn – turn left **Ⓐ** on to a path across West Heath. Head downhill through woodland into a dip and, before emerging on to a road, bear right to continue along the left edge of the heath. The path later continues beside West Heath Road to a broad track.

Turn right **Ⓑ** along this track (Sandy Road), pass to the left of a pond called the Leg of Mutton and head gently uphill to reach a tarmac drive. Continue along it, going round a left bend, to a road opposite the Old Bull and Bush, another old pub, made famous in a Victorian music-hall song. Turn right, almost immediately turn left along North End **Ⓒ** and, where the road ends, pass beside a barrier and continue along

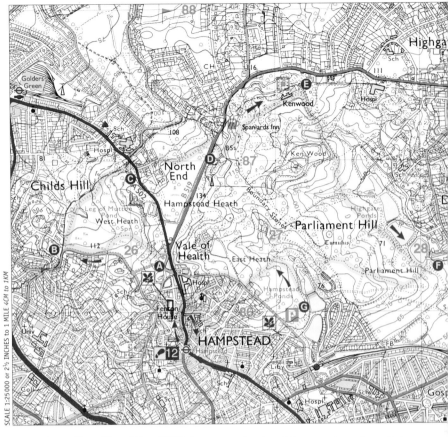

SCALE 1:25 000 or 2½ INCHES to 1 MILE 4CM to 1KM

```
0      200    400    600    800 METRES    1
                                          KILOMETRES
                                          MILES
0      200    400    600 YARDS    ½
```

a track through the woodland of Sandy Heath. Keep on the main, broad track all the time, which bears left and continues to a road. About 100 yds (91m) to the left is the Spaniards Inn, the third of the trio of traditional heath pubs, a mainly 18th-century building. It claims to date back to 1585 and to have been frequented by Dick Turpin.

Turn right along Spaniards Inn Road and after a few yards turn left through a gate on to an enclosed path **D**. Take the left-hand, downhill path at a fork, which curves left through the trees to another fork. Again take the left-hand path, which continues down to reach a clear, well-surfaced track at a junction. Continue along the track straight ahead, which meanders across open grassland,

bearing right to go through a gate to a T-junction.

Turn left on to a broad track, which bears right to continue across the terrace in front of Kenwood House. This elegant 18th-century mansion, designed by Robert Adam for the Earl of Mansfield, was bequeathed to the nation in 1927 by Edward Guinness, Earl of Iveagh. The 'Iveagh Bequest' included the grounds, a popular venue for outdoor concerts in the summer, and his superb collection of paintings.

At a fork at the end of the terrace, take the right-hand track **E**, which curves right and descends, passing to the left of a lake. Keep ahead through woodland, by a wire fence on the right, and go through a metal gate to a cross-way on the edge of open heathland again. Continue along the tarmac track in front, take the left-hand path at a fork and pass through a belt of trees to a track. Keep ahead along a grassy path, heading gently uphill, and at a fork just over the slight rise take the left-hand path, which descends to a tarmac path.

Turn left and follow it along the right edge of two of the series of Highgate Ponds; the path soon broadens out into a wide track. At a junction by the end of the last pond, turn sharp right **F** on to a gently ascending path. At the next junction continue along the right-hand path and follow it up to the top of Parliament Hill. Despite a modest height of 320ft (98m), the views, both the nearer ones across to Hampstead and Highgate villages and the wider ones over London, are outstanding. A viewfinder identifies all the places that can

be seen from here in clear conditions.

Keep ahead past the viewfinder, descending towards woodland, and continue through the trees. The path continues to descend and crosses a causeway between two of the Hampstead Ponds. Head uphill for about 50 yds (46m) and turn sharp right **G** on to a path along the right edge of grassland, later entering woodland and climbing steps to reach a track. This is the Boundary Path, and you turn left along this beautiful, tree-lined track to emerge on to East Heath Road.

Turn right uphill, turn left into Cannon Place and pass to the right of Christ Church. Bear left through Hampstead Square, turn right along Elm Row to a T-junction and turn left down Heath Street to the start. ●

Hampstead Heath – around 790 acres (320ha) of hills and valleys rising to 440ft (134m)

Blackheath and Greenwich Park

Start	Blackheath Station
Distance	5 miles (8km)
Approximate time	2½ hours
Parking	Blackheath Station (there are other car parks in Blackheath)
Refreshments	Pubs and cafés at Blackheath; cafés in Greenwich Park; pubs and cafés at Greenwich
Public transport	Trains from London (Charing Cross) to Blackheath
Ordnance Survey maps	Landranger 177 (East London, Billericay & Gravesend), Explorer 162 (Greenwich & Gravesend)

The first and last parts of the walk are across Blackheath; most of the remainder is a circuit of Greenwich Park, passing the Old Royal Observatory, National Maritime Museum and Royal Naval College buildings. From the higher points in the park, the superb views include Greenwich below and the great sweep of the River Thames, with St Paul's Cathedral, Canary Wharf and the Millennium Dome on the skyline. The route also includes a walk under the Greenwich Foot Tunnel to Island Gardens on the Isle of Dogs in order to experience the classic view of Greenwich, looking back across the river to the complex of buildings, with the park rising behind them.

Turn left out of the station, take the right-hand road at a fork and take the first turning on the left up to the heath. Because of its location astride the main approach to London from Dover and the continent, Blackheath has witnessed a number of stirring national events over the centuries. Wat Tyler and his rebels assembled here to meet Richard II during the Peasants' Revolt in 1381. A later rebel force, led by Jack Cade, also met here in 1450. Henry VII defeated Cornish rebels on the heath in 1497. Henry V was welcomed here in 1415 after his triumph at Agincourt, and

Charles II entered his capital from Blackheath at the Restoration of the Monarchy in 1660.

Cross a road and continue along All Saints' Drive, passing to the left of All Saints Church. Keep ahead along a tarmac path across the heath, take the right-hand path at a fork and continue to a road. Bear right along it to cross a road, keep ahead to cross another one and continue along Duke Humphrey Road. After crossing another road, you enter Greenwich Park by Blackheath Gate **A**. This is the oldest of the royal parks, enclosed by Humphrey Duke of

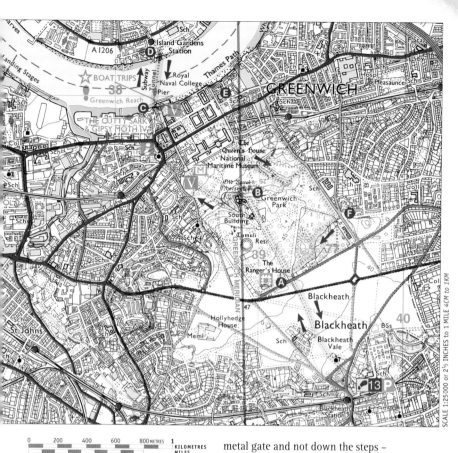

SCALE 1:25000 or 2½ INCHES to 1 MILE 4CM to 1KM

0	200	400	600	800 METRES	1

KILOMETRES
MILES

0	200	400	600 YARDS	½

Gloucester, uncle of Henry VI, in 1433.

Keep straight ahead along a tree-lined road to the Old Royal Observatory and the statue to General Wolfe **B**. From here the view over Greenwich, the River Thames, the Millennium Dome and the London skyline is magnificent. Charles II founded the Royal Observatory in 1675 for the study of astronomy and marine navigation. Later the Prime Meridian Line, 0° longitude, was positioned here, giving visitors the unusual experience of being able to stand with one foot in the western hemisphere and the other in the eastern hemisphere. The Royal Observatory buildings are now part of the National Maritime Museum.

At a fork just beyond the statue, take the left-hand path – going through a metal gate and not down the steps – which crosses the Greenwich Meridian Line, curves left in front of the observatory and descends to a park road. Turn right downhill, leave the park by St Mary's Gate and keep ahead along King William Walk into Greenwich. Turn left along Nelson Road to St Alfege's Church, built by Hawksmoor in 1714 and restored after bomb damage in the Second World War, and turn right along Greenwich Church Street. Turn right again into College Approach and, in front of the gates of the Royal Naval College, turn left to Greenwich Pier and the *Cutty Sark* **C**. This grand old sailing-ship was the last and fastest of the tea-clippers.

Turn left by the pier to a circular, domed brick building. This is the entrance to the Greenwich Foot Tunnel, opened in 1902, which takes you under the Thames to emerge at Island

Gardens. Turn right for the classic view across the river at Greenwich **D**. Apart from the Old Royal Observatory on the hill, this uniquely imposing and grandiose complex of Classical buildings comprises the Royal Naval College, the Queen's House and the National Maritime Museum. Its building history and variety of roles is quite complicated. The original medieval manor-house was rebuilt by Henry VII, and it was in this palace, called Placentia, that Henry VIII, Mary I and Elizabeth I were all born. In the early 17th century, Inigo Jones was commissioned to build the Queen's House, regarded as the first Classical building in England, for the wife of James I, although it was completed for Henrietta Maria, Charles I's wife. In the 1660s, Charles II demolished the Tudor palace and began the construction of a new one but the site of this was later donated by Mary II as a hospital for seamen. Wren was the architect for this Royal Naval Hospital but it was not completed until long after his death. In 1873 it changed its role to become the Royal Naval College, and the Queen's House and adjoining buildings became the National Maritime Museum in 1933. At present the future of the college is

Looking across the River Thames to Canary Wharf from the Royal Observatory at Greenwich

again in doubt as the Ministry of Defence no longer need it and are about to vacate the buildings.

Retrace your steps under the Thames to Greenwich and turn left alongside the river, following Thames Path signs. Pass in front of the Royal Naval College, turn right, between the college on your right and the Trafalgar Tavern, a traditional riverside pub, on your left, and take the first turning on the left **E** for a short detour along the Thames Path to a garden area in front of Trinity Hospital, an almshouse founded in 1613. The hospital is dwarfed by the adjacent power-station.

Return to the Trafalgar Tavern, turn left to continue along Park Row, cross the main road and keep ahead alongside the Queen's House to re-enter the park. Take the broad path ahead, passing to the right of a children's boating-pool, and at a junction of paths, bear left, in the 'Flower Garden and Deer Enclosure' direction, along another broad, tree-lined path. Head uphill, passing to the right of a mound and, at a crossway, turn left on to a narrower path, which continues up to Maze Hill Gate. The brick-built house just to the left on the other side of the road is Vanbrugh Castle, designed by Vanbrugh and his home from 1719 to 1726.

Don't go through the gate but turn right to follow a path alongside the park wall to a junction of paths by Vanbrugh Park Gate **F**. At this junction, turn half-right – not sharp right – in the 'Flower Garden and Deer Enclosure' direction again, and walk through the Flower Garden to a T-junction. The Deer Park is over to the left. Turn left, go across the Flower Garden, and the path curves right, passes a pond and goes through a metal gate on to the main park road.

Turn left through Blackheath Gate **A**, here picking up the outward route, and retrace your steps to the start. ●

Hampton Court and Bushy parks

Start	Hampton Court Station on south side of Hampton Court Bridge
Distance	5½ miles (8.9km)
Approximate time	2½ hours
Parking	Hampton Court Station
Refreshments	Pubs and cafés at Hampton Court; tearoom at Hampton Court Palace; pubs at Hampton Wick; kiosk near the Diana Fountain in Bushy Park
Public transport	Trains from London (Waterloo) to Hampton Court
Ordnance Survey maps	Landranger 176 (West London), Explorer 161 (London South, Croydon & Esher)

Inevitably the chief focal point of the walk is the magnificent Hampton Court Palace, the nearest England has to Versailles, and there are some memorable views of it on the first part of the route. From the palace and its ornamental gardens, the walk heads across Hampton Court Park to the banks of the River Thames and then follows the river to Kingston Bridge. The return to Hampton Court is across the wide and open expanses of the adjacent Bushy Park. Deer are likely to be seen in both parks.

Start by crossing Hampton Court Bridge, turn right through the gates of the palace and walk along a broad drive, parallel to the river. Hampton Court Palace is really two palaces in one: the original redbrick Tudor palace, built by Cardinal Wolsey and altered by Henry VIII, and the elegant late-17th-century extension designed by Wren for William III and Mary II. The contrast between the two halves is quite striking.

The palace was built by Wolsey in 1514 and given to Henry VIII in 1525 in a desperate but unsuccessful attempt to keep in favour with the King. It became Henry's favourite residence. He built the Great Hall, noted for its superb hammer-beam roof, two of his marriages took

place here, and his third wife, Jane Seymour, died in the palace in 1537 shortly after giving birth to the future Edward VI. Over a century later, following the accession to the throne of William III and Mary II in 1689, Wren was entrusted with building an extension that would turn Hampton Court into an English Versailles. William and Mary were also responsible for the ornamental gardens; the Maze – a popular attraction with visitors – was created a little later in the reign of Queen Anne.

Turn left in front of Wolsey's Great Gatehouse, go under an arch, keep ahead along the right edge of gardens and turn right through a gate Ⓐ.

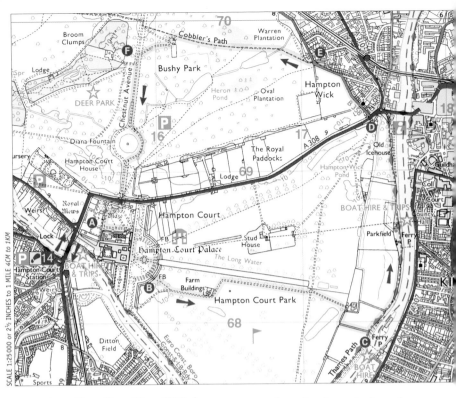

SCALE 1:25000 or 2½ INCHES to 1 MILE 4CM to 1KM

<table>
<tr><td>0</td><td>200</td><td>400</td><td>600</td><td>800 METRES</td><td>1</td><td>KILOMETRES</td></tr>
<tr><td></td><td></td><td></td><td></td><td></td><td></td><td>MILES</td></tr>
<tr><td>0</td><td>200</td><td>400</td><td>600 YARDS</td><td></td><td>½</td><td></td></tr>
</table>

Continue along a straight path, sign-posted 'Vine and Toilets', go through a gate and turn right to walk along the east front of the palace, part of Wren's 17th-century extension. Turn left towards a fountain, and beyond that is the start of the Long Water, created for Charles II shortly after the Restoration, possibly as a reminder of Holland, where he had spent his exile. At a statue just in front of the lake, turn right, turn left to cross a footbridge **B** and go through wrought-iron gates into the park.

The path bears left to join a tarmac track. Continue along it, turning left by farm buildings and bending right to continue alongside Long Water. Where the lake ends, keep ahead at a crossing of tracks and shortly bear right off the track along a grassy path that skirts the left edge of Rick Pond and continues to

a metal gate in a fence. Go through, walk along a fence-lined path and go through another metal gate to the River Thames **C**.

Turn left on to the riverside path – it later becomes a wide tarmac track – and follow it for ¾ mile (1.2km) to Kingston Bridge. At the bridge, turn left into Hampton Wick, follow the road to the left and turn right into Church Grove **D**, signposted to Teddington. The road bears left and, where it bends right, turn left through a metal gate to enter Bushy Park **E**. The tarmac path, Cobbler's Path, which you take across the park, gets its name from a local shoemaker, Timothy Bennet, who threatened court action against the Earl of Halifax, the park ranger, when he closed the path in 1752. Halifax backed down, and the path has remained a public right of way ever since. At the entrance to the park is a memorial to Timothy Bennet.

After crossing a narrow stream, bear left and continue along the path until you reach a fence on the left. Bear left on to a grassy path, which follows the curve of the fence round to the left to join a tarmac path by a house. Take the second – not the first – path on the right, which bears slightly left to the Chestnut Avenue **F**. This was planned by Wren as a grand approach to a new northern façade to Hampton Court Palace, which was never built. Turn left beside the avenue, continue past the imposing Diana Fountain and leave the park by the Hampton Court Gate.

Go through the Lion Gate opposite to re-enter Hampton Court Park and, at a meeting of paths ahead, take the one to the right, passing to the left of the Maze. Turn left at a T-junction in front of the tearoom and at a crossing of paths rejoin the outward route to retrace your steps to the start. ●

Hampton Court Palace

Enfield Chase

Start	Trent Country Park
Distance	4 miles (6.4km). Add ¾ mile (1.2km) if coming from Cockfosters Station
Approximate time	2 hours (2½ hours from Cockfosters)
Parking	Trent Country Park
Refreshments	Café by car park
Public transport	Underground to Cockfosters (Piccadilly line). Turn right along the main road, turn right through the entrance to Trent Country Park and follow the drive to the car park
Ordnance Survey maps	Landranger 166 (Luton & Hertford), Explorer 173 (London North, Harrow & Enfield)

Trent Country Park is a remnant of the ancient royal hunting-ground of Enfield Chase, which once extended over nearly 8000 acres (3238ha) of north Middlesex, part of the extensive woodlands that surrounded much of the capital. This easy paced walk is a pleasant mixture of woodland and grassland and includes a lake, water gardens and a glimpse of Trent House, now part of Middlesex University.

The walk starts in the car park, at the information board by the café. Walk back along the drive, go through the gates of the car park and, just beyond a monument (which informs you that the gardens were begun in 1706) and a 'Welcome to Trent Country Park' board, turn left, at a London Loop footpath post. Head across the grass to the next post and continue along the left edge of a field, by woodland on the left. Bear left into the wood – Church Wood – follow a winding path through it, turn right at a footpath post and bear left to emerge from the trees.

Keep ahead across a field, cross a footbridge over a ditch and, at the next London Loop post, turn left – here leaving the 'Loop' – and walk along the left edge of a field. Continue through a line of trees and on across the next field, heading gently downhill. In the field corner, turn

In Trent Country Park

left **Ⓐ** on to a path that gently ascends along the right, inside edge of Church Wood and turn right at a T-junction along a straight, tree-lined path.

At a gate, turn left along a path to reach a tarmac drive, by an information centre **Ⓑ**, cross it and keep ahead, in the Lakes and Water Garden direction, along a track through woodland. The track later emerges into open country and bears right to keep parallel to the edge of a lake. At a fork **Ⓒ** take the right-hand track – for a short detour to the Water Garden – and Trent House can be seen to the right above the lake.

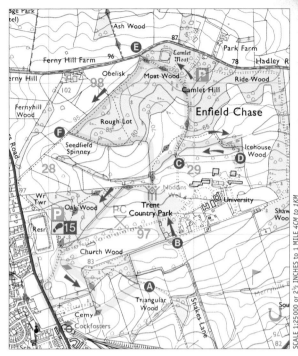

The house has certainly had a variety of roles. Originally a small 18th-century villa, it was rebuilt on a more grandiose scale by the Sassoon family in the early 20th century. During the Second World War it was used as an interrogation centre for high-ranking German prisoners and now it is part of Middlesex University.

The path curves right alongside the lake, and you go through a gate into the Water Garden **Ⓓ**. This was developed by Sir Philip Sassoon and after being neglected in the Second World War was restored and reopened in 1984. Retrace your steps to the fork **Ⓒ** and turn right along a broad, gently ascending track through woodland, following London Loop waymarks again. Keep along the edge of the trees for a while before continuing through this delightful woodland again. Take the left-hand track at a fork, at a T-junction turn left, ignore a London Loop sign to the right and continue to another T-junction on

the edge of the trees a few yards ahead **Ⓔ**. Turn left, passing an obelisk, and continue through the wood.

At the corner of the wood, follow the track to the left **Ⓕ** and head gently downhill along the right inside edge of the wood – or alternatively along a parallel path along its right edge – and at the edge of the trees, turn right along the right edge of open grassland, by a hedge on the right, heading down to a T-junction. Turn right, here briefly rejoining the outward route and, at a London Loop post by a Trent Country Park notice-board, turn right on to a path, by a hedge on the right.

At the corner of Oak Wood, turn left and keep alongside the left edge of the trees up to a tarmac drive. Turn right alongside it and head towards the monument that was passed at the start of the walk and, just before reaching it, turn right along a tarmac path into the car park. ●

Little Venice, Regent's Park and Primrose Hill

Start	Little Venice
Distance	5½ miles (8.9km). Shorter version 5 miles (8km)
Approximate time	3 hours (2½ hours for shorter walk)
Refreshments	Cafés at Little Venice; pub and café *en route*; café in Regent's Park
Public transport	Underground to Warwick Avenue (Bakerloo line). Walk along Warwick Avenue to the crossroads, and Little Venice is to the right
Ordnance Survey maps	Landranger 176 (West London), Explorer 173 (London North, Harrow & Enfield)

From the canal basin at Little Venice, the walk proceeds beside an attractive stretch of the Regent's Canal to Regent's Park. This is followed by a circuit of this superb park, including a visit to the ornamental Queen Mary's Gardens. A short detour to the summit of Primrose Hill provides a grand panoramic view over London. The shorter walk omits this detour and returns directly to Little Venice along the canal.

Little Venice, the nickname given to the canal basin just to the north of Paddington Station, is the starting point of both the Grand Union and Regent's canals. It is a most attractive area, with colourful gardens and leafy roads, lined with handsome and dignified Victorian houses along the canal banks. The Regent's Canal was opened in 1820 and runs from here to Limehouse Basin, completing the link between Birmingham and the Thames.

Start by walking along Blomfield Road, with the canal on the right, cross Warwick Avenue and continue along the tree-lined left bank of the canal up to Edgware Road **A**. At this point the Regent's Canal disappears into the Maida Vale tunnel. Keep ahead along Aberdeen Place and, where the road

turns left, take the path in front and descend iron steps to rejoin the canal. Walk along the towpath, going first under a tunnel and then under foot, rail and road bridges in quick succession. The greenery of Regent's Park can be seen over to the right.

After passing under the next bridge (Charlbert Bridge) **B**, turn left up a path, turn sharp left and then left again to cross the bridge, cross a road and go through Charlbert Bridge Gate into Regent's Park. In the Middle Ages this area was part of the Forest of Middlesex but in the 16th century it was acquired by Henry VIII, who converted it into the royal hunting-ground of Marylebone Park. It assumed its present form in the early 19th century when John Nash transformed this part of London and

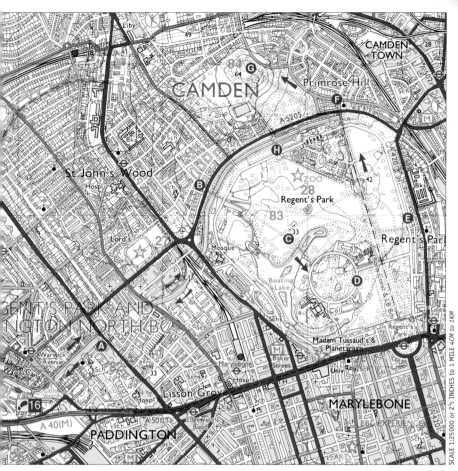

surrounded the park with elegant terraces. London Zoo occupies part of the north side of the park, and to the west is the London Mosque.

Take the right-hand path at a fork and at the next fork take the right-hand path again to reach the end of the boating-lake. Continue along the left edge of the lake as it curves left, turn right **C** to cross a footbridge over it and keep ahead through Longbridge Gate on to the Inner Circle. This road encircles the Inner Park or Queen Mary's Gardens. Turn left and follow the curve of the circle to the right to Chester Road Gate **D**, where you can enter the colourful and attractive Queen Mary's Gardens, predominantly a rose garden set amidst a small ornamental lake.

0	200	400	600	800 metres	1
					KILOMETRES
					MILES
0	200	400	600 yards	½	

Returning to the Chester Road Gate, keep ahead along Chester Road and, at a pedestrian crossing, turn left into Broad Walk, a wide, straight, tree-lined drive. Immediately turn right off it on to a path that bears left to Cumberland Gate **E** in order to take a look at Cumberland Terrace – across the road on the left – probably the most impressive of the Regency terraces built around the park by Nash. Re-enter the park and take the path to the right of your previous path to rejoin the Broad Walk. Turn right along it, later keeping along the right edge of London Zoo, go through a gate to leave the park and cross first a road and then the canal bridge to reach another road, Prince Albert Road **F**.

If you wish to omit the detour to Primrose Hill, turn right, then sharp right, at a footpath sign, to descend to the canal towpath and keep along it, picking up the full walk at point **H**.

For the full walk, turn left to the corner of Albert Terrace, where you enter Primrose Hill, acquired as an extension to Regent's Park in 1841. At a fork take the right-hand path, which heads gently uphill and curves left to the viewfinder at the top **G**. Although only 219ft (64m) high, the views over London are superb and take in many major landmarks, including the dome of St Paul's and, inevitably, Canary Wharf tower.

Keep ahead past the viewfinder along a path that curves left downhill to join a straight path and continue along it to emerge on to Prince Albert Road again. Turn right and, at a public footpath sign 'Canalside Walk', turn left towards the canal. Just before reaching the bridge, turn right onto a hedge-lined path, which turns sharp left and then sharp right on to the towpath **H**. Here you pick up the outward route and retrace your steps to the start.

Little Venice, Paddington

Hainault Forest

Start	Hainault Forest Country Park, first car park near the refreshment kiosk
Distance	5 miles (8km). Add 3½ miles (5.6km) if coming from Grange Hill Station and pick up the walk at point **G**
Approximate time	2½ hours (4 hours from Grange Hill Station)
Parking	Hainault Forest Country Park
Refreshments	Kiosk at start; pub at Lambourne End
Public transport	Underground to Grange Hill. Turn right along Manor Road, turn right at traffic lights and at the next set of traffic lights (by the Oak pub), turn left through a fence gap into the country park and follow a path to the lake, where you join the main route at point **G**
Ordnance Survey maps	Landranger 177 (East London, Billericay & Gravesend), Explorer 174 (Epping Forest & Lee Valley)

Although a smaller remnant of the ancient Forest of Essex than Epping, Hainault Forest is nevertheless a superb remnant with expanses of open grassland combined with some outstandingly beautiful woodland. Considering that the forest is on the doorstep of north-east London – Canary Wharf tower is visible at times – the views over the Essex countryside from its eastern and northern fringes are surprisingly peaceful and rural. This is a figure-of-eight walk, with a pub approximately half-way round.

Hainault Forest, originally part of the vast forest of Essex, was held by the abbots of Barking until the dissolution of the monasteries, when it was acquired by Henry VIII. It remained Crown property until 1851, after which the forest was enclosed and much of it felled. What remained was bought by London County Council in 1903 as a recreation area, and it has subsequently become a popular country park.

Start by facing the refreshment kiosk and turn left along the tarmac drive, passing to the left of Foxburrows Farm, now a rare-breeds centre, and the buildings of the Country Park Office. Where the drive ends in front of the gates of a golf-course, turn left **A**

along a tree-lined path that bears slightly right and heads gently uphill into woodland. At a junction of paths by a Hainault Forest Country Park notice, keep ahead into the trees and after about 100 yds (91m) turn right at a crossing of paths **B**.

Continue through beautiful woodland, at a fork take the left-hand path, heading gently downhill to cross a tiny brook, and eventually you go through a kissing-gate to a T-junction near the edge of the forest. Turn right uphill, passing to the right of houses, to a footpath post **C**. At this point a brief detour ahead leads to a fine view over the tranquil and gently rolling Essex countryside.

A pathway through Hainault Forest

At the footpath post, turn left to climb a stile and walk along a grassy path enclosed between wire fences to another stile. Climb that, continue gently uphill along the right edge of a field and in the top corner, cross a plank footbridge over a ditch on to a road. Turn left and at a junction turn right along New Road, signposted to Abridge, through Lambourne End. Where the road bends right, turn left over a stile

D at a public footpath sign, walk along a track and bear right downhill along the right edge of a field. Climb a stile, continue downhill and climb another stile on to a lane.

Turn left and follow the undulating lane to a T-junction beside the Camelot pub **E**. Cross over, keep ahead through a car park and pass beside a barrier to re-enter the Country Park. Continue through more delightful woodland to the crossway passed earlier **B** and keep ahead for about 100 yds (91m) – briefly

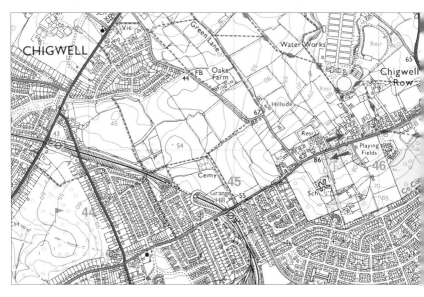

joining the outward route. On emerging from the trees, turn right. Immediately take the left-hand path at a fork and turn left at a white-waymarked post **F**.

Turn right at a crossway, and the path heads gently downhill, winding along the left, inside edge of woodland. From here there are fine views across the open grassland to the left, with the tower of Canary Wharf visible on the horizon. Look out for a crossing of paths – just before crossing a brook – where you turn left. Take the right-hand path at a fork and continue along the right edge of the lake for a pleasant finale to the walk, following the curve of the lake round to the left **G**.

Walkers returning to Grange Hill turn right here to pick up the outward route and retrace their steps to the station.

The path heads back along the other side of the lake and bends right to return to the start. ●

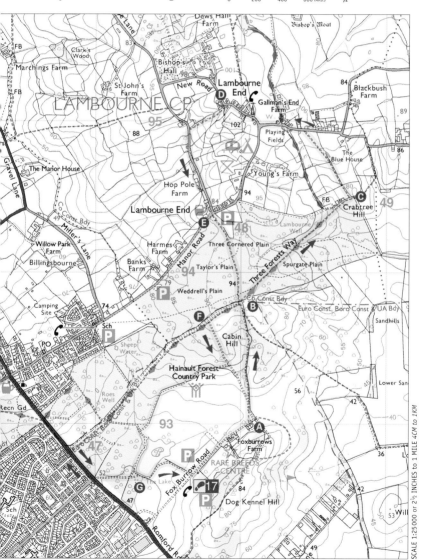

SCALE 1:25000 or 2½ INCHES to 1 MILE 4CM to 1KM

Marden Park Woods

Start	Woldingham Station
Distance	4½ miles (7.2km). Shorter version 2½ miles (4km)
Approximate time	2 hours (1 hour for the shorter walk)
Parking	Woldingham Station
Refreshments	None
Public transport	Trains from London (Victoria) to Woldingham
Ordnance Survey maps	Landranger 187 (Dorking, Reigate & Crawley), Explorer 146 (Dorking, Box Hill & Reigate)

Much of this well-waymarked walk is through the attractive Marden Park Woods, from where there are fine views over the Marden valley and rolling chalk downland. A short stretch of the North Downs Way is used, and from here you look southwards across the well-wooded ridges and valleys of the Weald. There is also the chance to visit the highest, and certainly one of the smallest, churches in Surrey.

Turn right out of the station car park along Church Road, which keeps parallel to the railway line. The road becomes a rough track, and you continue along it as far as a public footpath sign, just before reaching woodland **A**. Turn right down to a stile, climb it and turn left on to an enclosed path above a steep cutting.

The path turns right to cross the railway line and continues to another stile. Climb it, turn left and head steadily uphill through the trees to reach a T-junction **B**.

*If doing the short walk, turn right and head downhill, still through woodland, to a junction of tracks **F**, where you turn right again, in the Woldingham Station direction, to rejoin the full walk.*

For the full walk, turn left uphill, take the left-hand track at a fork and continue up to a kissing-gate on the right that admits you to Great Church Wood **C**. A brief detour ahead leads to the attractive, early-19th-century St Agatha's Church. At 775ft (236m),

this is the highest church in Surrey; it may also possibly be the smallest.

The route continues, via the kissing-gate, along a path through Great Church Wood, which like much of Marden Park Woods is now owned by the Woodland Trust. The path curves right downhill and eventually descends a flight of steps to a track. Turn left, head uphill through Marden Park Wood, go through a gate and on through South Hawke car park to a lane. Turn right, almost immediately turn left down steps and, at a T-junction, turn right along a path, here joining the North Downs Way **D**. On this section of the route, gaps in the trees on the left reveal grand and extensive views across the Weald, but the noise from the M25 immediately below is inescapable. Follow the regular North Downs Way signs, curving right and then turning left, and the tree-lined path later runs parallel to the lane and eventually emerges on to it. Walk along the lane

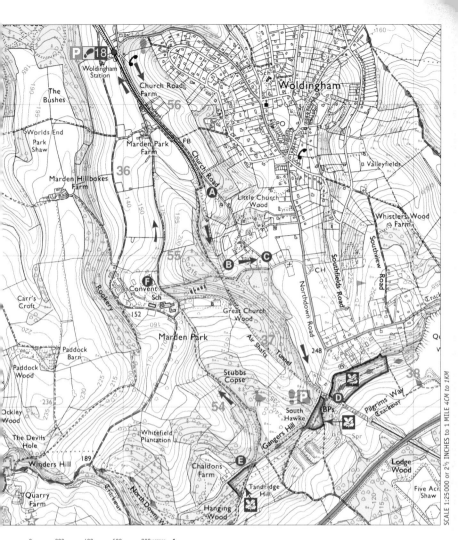

SCALE 1:25000 or 2½ INCHES to 1 MILE 4CM to 1KM

0 200 400 600 800 METRES 1 KILOMETRES MILES
0 200 400 600 YARDS ½

and turn right through a gate **E** at a Woodland Trust notice, into another part of Marden Park Wood.

The track bears left, later narrows to a path and continues through this beautiful area of woodland, following the regular 'Woldingham Country Walk' waymarks. Climb a stile to emerge from the trees, head downhill along the left edge of the wood and, at the bottom, climb another stile on to a tarmac drive. To the left is Marden Park, an imposing Victorian country-house built in the 1880s. Since the Second World War it

has been used as a boarding-school.

Continue, passing between the school buildings on the left and a cemetery on the right, and the tarmac drive becomes a rough track that heads uphill between embankments to a junction of tracks **F**. Keep ahead – here rejoining the short walk – in the Woldingham Station direction along an enclosed, tree- and hedge-lined track, enjoying the views to the left over the beautiful and secluded Marden valley. The track descends to a farm. Keep ahead. The track becomes a tarmac one that bends right and crosses the railway line to a T-junction. Turn left, rejoining the outward route, and follow Church Road back to the start. ●

Banstead Wood and Park Downs

Start	Chipstead, Holly Lane car park
Distance	4½ miles (7.2km). Add ½ mile (800m) if coming from Chipstead Station
Approximate time	2 hours (2¼ hours from Chipstead Station)
Parking	Holly Lane car park
Refreshments	Sometimes a kiosk at the start
Public transport	Trains from London (Victoria) to Chipstead. Turn left out of the station and follow a road to the right down to the main road. Turn left, take the first turning on the right – Lower Park Road – and the car park is about 100 yds (91m) along on the left
Ordnance Survey maps	Landranger 187 (Dorking, Reigate & Crawley), Explorer 146 (Dorking, Box Hill & Reigate)

There is a surprisingly remote feel on parts of this well-waymarked walk, despite being almost enveloped by suburban Surrey and not far from the M25. The route begins by following the edge of Banstead Wood, an ancient woodland with a wide range of animal and plant species. On this stretch there are fine views over the Chipstead valley. It then heads across more open country to continue through the attractive woodland and chalk downland of Park Downs, which is an area of common land managed by a board of conservators.

With your back to the road, make for the top left corner of the car park and go through a kissing-gate. Take the path ahead and, at a fingerpost by a junction of paths and tracks, follow a track into the woodland, in the direction of a public footpath sign to Perrotts Farm. At the next footpath sign a few yards ahead, continue along the left edge of Banstead Wood, following the signs for the Banstead Country Walk. The path heads uphill and soon re-enters the wood; to the left the views over the Chipstead valley are most attractive.

At a fork by a fingerpost, keep ahead, in the 'Summer Route' direction, along a path that contours along a wooded hillside. Continue along the right edge of trees, in the Fames Rough direction, cross a track and keep ahead to re-enter the wood, following the regular Banstead Country Walk signs all the while. The path bears right and ascends gently to a T-junction. Turn left, in the 'Main Route' direction, then keep ahead at the next footpath sign and the path curves right to head up to a stile.

Climb the stile, continue along the left edge of the wood towards a farm

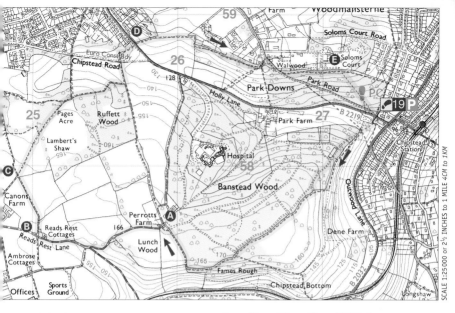

and climb another stile in the field corner Ⓐ. Turn left on to a track, at a public bridleway sign to Burgh Heath, pass in front of the farmhouse and continue along the broad track that bends right towards the next farm. At a crossing of tracks just beyond this farm – where there is a public footpath sign to Banstead – turn right Ⓑ through a gate and keep ahead along a track to a stile.

Climb the stile, continue along the left edge of a field and at a public footpath sign to Holly Lane Ⓒ turn right across the field towards trees. Climb a stile on the far side, continue through the trees and then bear left along the left edge of a field to climb another stile. Walk along the right, inside edge of woodland, bear right on joining another path, climb a stile and keep ahead along the left edge of Ruffett Wood, descending to a T-junction.

Turn left, in the Park Downs direction, climb a stile in the field corner and keep ahead through trees, curving right to

At the edge of Banstead Wood

emerge on to a road Ⓓ. Cross over, climb the stile opposite and walk along the left edge of a field. Follow the field edge to the right and, at a footpath post, turn left over a stile. Continue along an attractive, tree-lined path and at a fork take the left-hand path, which heads over Park Downs along the edge of the trees. Later the path enters woodland to reach a crossway.

Keep ahead, in the Park Road direction, cross a lane and take the path ahead through more delightful woodland. At a fork, continue along the left-hand path and look out for a footpath post, where you turn right Ⓔ on to a path that winds downhill through the trees to emerge into a more open, grassy area. Bear left, immediately turn right, by a Banstead Country Walk sign, and the path continues down to Holly Lane opposite the car park. ●

SCALE 1:25000 or 2½ INCHES to 1 MILE 4CM to 1KM

| 0 | 200 | 400 | 600 | 800 METRES | 1 |
| 0 | 200 | 400 | 600 YARDS | ½ |

KILOMETRES
MILES

Ruislip Woods and Lido

Start	Ruislip Lido
Distance	5½ miles (8.9km). Add 1¼ miles (2km) if coming from Ruislip Manor Station and pick up the walk at point **G**
Approximate time	3 hours (3½ hours from Ruislip Manor Station)
Parking	Ruislip Lido
Refreshments	Pub by Ruislip Lido
Public transport	Underground to Ruislip Manor (Metropolitan Line). Turn right and join the main route just after crossing the bridge over the River Pinn at point **G**
Ordnance Survey maps	Landranger 176 (West London), Explorers 172 (Chiltern Hills East, High Wycombe, Maidenhead) and 173 (London North, Harrow & Enfield)

Much of this route is through the attractive woodlands, remnants of the old Forest of Middlesex, that lie between Ruislip and Northwood, with a foray into suburban Ruislip for a walk across meadows bordering the little River Pinn. Towards the end come grand views across Ruislip Lido. You need to take careful heed of the route directions through Ruislip Woods as most of the paths are not waymarked.

From the car park entrance by the Waters Edge pub, go through a gate, at a Hillingdon Trail waymark, and walk along a well-constructed path across meadowland. At the next Hillingdon Trail sign, bear left across the grass and go through a gate into Copse Wood.

The path curves left at a Hillingdon Trail footpath post but at the next post turn right **A** to leave the Hillingdon Trail and continue gently uphill through this delightful area of woodland. Turn right at a T-junction, almost immediately turn left and keep in a straight line, heading gently downhill to pass through a barrier to a T-junction on the edge of the wood **B**. Turn right to emerge on to the end of a road and turn right on to a path that re-enters the wood.

Look out for a path on the left that winds through the trees down to a fence and kissing-gate. Don't go through the gate but turn left on to a fence-lined path that keeps along the right, inside edge of the wood. Keep ahead at a crossway, bear left and cross a small brook to emerge on to the edge of a golf-course. Turn right **C** along a path that winds along the left, inside edge of the trees, follows the edge of the trees to the left and continues along the right edge of the golf-course.

Turn sharp right to cross a footbridge over a brook, continue along the left edge of woodland, by a high wire fence on the right, bear left and then turn right to follow the path into Park Wood. Continue in a more or less straight line through the wood and soon you see a

0	200	400	600	800 METRES	1
					KILOMETRES
					MILES
0	200	400	600 YARDS	½	

miniature railway line beyond a wire
fence on the right. Just after the path
bears slightly right, turn left **D** to
continue along a clear, straight, steadily
ascending path. The path later levels off
and then gently descends to a major
junction of paths and tracks. Cross a
small brook, keep ahead gently uphill
again and after about 100 yds (91m)
another path comes in from the right.
At this point turn left **E** to pick up the

path seen ahead and follow it to a stile
on the edge of the trees.

Climb the stile and bear right across
grass to follow a broad and obvious
path into the trees again. The path bears
left and then curves right to emerge, via
a barrier, on to a suburban road. Keep
ahead to a T-junction, turn left along
Elmbridge Drive and just after a right
bend – and before a bridge – turn right
through a fence gap **F** and walk along
a path across meadows beside the little
River Pinn. Pass through a line of trees,
continue along the edge of the next

stretch of meadowland and keep ahead to go through a metal gate on to a road .

Turn left here if returning to Ruislip Manor Station.

Turn right and just before a road junction, turn left through a metal gate on to a track and turn left again to pass in front of an abandoned sports pavilion. Turn right along a path across fields, by a wire fence on the right, follow the path to the left and, where it bends left again, turn sharp right and go through a hedge gap to continue alongside the river again. At the end of the meadow, go through a metal gate on to a road, cross over and take the straight, paved path ahead.

On reaching the end of a road ⓗ, turn right along it (Sherwood Road), keep ahead at a crossroads, and at a T-junction pass through a barrier on to a path that re-enters Park Wood. At a fork take the right-hand path and, ignoring all side paths, follow it to a crossway. Keep ahead here, and the path bears slightly left to reach a T-junction in front of Ruislip Lido. Originally constructed in 1811 as a feeder reservoir for the Grand Junction – later Grand Union – Canal, the lido is now a popular and attractive recreational amenity.

Turn left along a path that keeps alongside a fence bordering the lido but look out for where you turn right through a fence gap to continue along a tarmac path across the end of the lido. Go through a gate on to a road and turn right to return to the start. ●

Ruislip Lido

Cassiobury Park and Whippendell Wood

Start	Watford, by the railway bridge in Gade Avenue, just off the A412 between Watford and Rickmansworth
Distance	6 miles (9.7km). Add ¾ mile (1.2km) if coming from Watford Station
Approximate time	3 hours (3½ hours from Watford Station)
Parking	Parking area by the railway bridge in Gade Avenue
Refreshments	Pub at Chandler's Cross
Public transport	Underground to Watford (Metropolitan line). Turn left along Cassiobury Park Drive, turn left into Swiss Avenue and continue along Gade Avenue to the parking area by the railway bridge
Ordnance Survey maps	Landranger 176 (West London), Explorer 172 (Chiltern Hills East, High Wycombe, Maidenhead)

This highly attractive and enjoyable woodland, parkland and waterside walk is not far from the centre of Watford. At both the start and finish there are pleasant stretches along the banks of the River Gade and the Grand Union Canal, with some delightful areas of woodland in between. As a bonus, there is a pub almost exactly half-way round.

Begin by taking the tarmac path along the right bank of the River Gade – it soon becomes a rough path – and follow it through Cassiobury Park, keeping by the attractive, tree-lined riverbank. This fine area of parkland was once the estate of the earls of Essex but the great house was demolished in 1927.

At a junction of paths by a footbridge, keep ahead along the middle tarmac path to a crossway in front of another footbridge. Turn right to rejoin the river, emerging-into more open parkland, pass a footbridge and keep to the left of a children's play and picnic area to reach a crossing of paths just to the right of another footbridge.

Turn left to cross first the river and then the Grand Union Canal, keep ahead to a fork by a footpath post and take the right-hand path **A** signposted public footpath 30. Keep along the main, tree-lined path all the while, initially just above the canal but then gradually bearing left away from it and heading gently uphill. After crossing several other paths, and part of the West Herts golf-course, look out for where the path passes some picnic tables.

At a fork just beyond the picnic tables **B** take the left-hand path, which descends through Whippendell Wood. Originally owned by the abbots of St Albans, this beautiful area of woodland passed to the earls of Essex

Whippendell Wood

following the dissolution of the monasteries in the 1530s. Like Cassiobury Park, it was later acquired for the people of Watford.

The multitude of paths through the wood can be confusing so it is important to take careful note of the following route directions. Keep ahead on the main path all the while until a fork where you take the right-hand path, passing through a glade and then into woodland again. Continue on the main path again – there are lots of side paths at this stage – and at a fork, just after the path starts to descend, keep along the wider right-hand path, which eventually emerges on to a lane **C**. Turn right along the narrow, tree-lined lane to a road and turn left into Chandler's Cross.

At a public footpath sign to Croxley Green, opposite the Clarendon Arms, turn left through a kissing-gate **D** and walk along a narrow, enclosed path. Pass through a fence gap to enter Harrocks Wood – owned by the Woodland Trust – and follow the path straight ahead through another delightful area of woodland. Climb a stile on the far side, continue along an enclosed path that emerges on to a track in front of a house and continue along the track as far as a public footpath sign by a barn **E**.

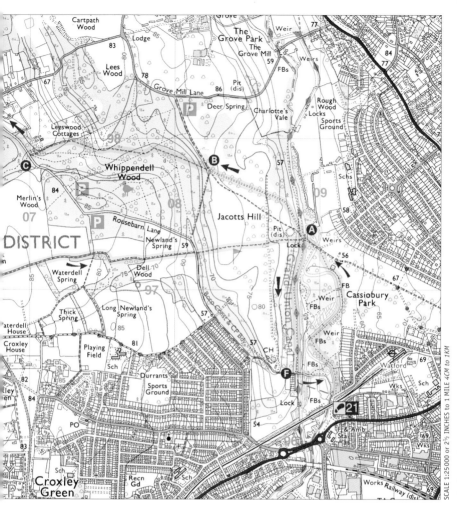

SCALE 1:25000 or 2½ INCHES to 1 MILE 4CM to 1KM

```
0      200    400    600    800 METRES  1
                                        KILOMETRES
                                        MILES
0      200    400    600 YARDS   ½
```

Turn left through a kissing-gate, in the Rousebarn Lane direction, walk along an enclosed path and climb a stile. Keep ahead along a track through a belt of trees. The track then narrows to a path that continues along the right edge of a field to a stile. Climb it, keep straight ahead across the next field towards woodland and go through a kissing-gate on to a lane. Take the path opposite, which heads uphill through trees to emerge on the edge of the West Herts golf-course again. The route continues in a straight line across the course, then through the next belt of trees, across another part of the course and finally down through more trees to the canal bridge **A**.

From here you could simply retrace your steps to the start but for an attractive and more interesting option, turn left in front of the bridge down to the towpath and turn sharp right to pass under it, by Ironbridge Lock. Walk along the tranquil, tree-lined towpath as far as the next bridge (No. 168) and bear right in front of it up to a track **F**.

Turn left to cross the bridge, continue along the track and at a fork take the left-hand path through woodland. Cross a footbridge over the River Gade and turn right to return to the starting point. ●

Epping Forest

Start	Epping Forest Museum (Queen Elizabeth's Hunting Lodge), on the A1069 to the east of Chingford
Distance	6 miles (9.7km). Add just over ½ mile (800m) if coming from Chingford Station
Approximate time	3 hours (3¼ hours from Chingford)
Parking	Epping Forest Museum
Refreshments	Pub and restaurant by Epping Forest Museum; pub at High Beach
Public transport	Trains from London (Liverpool Street) to Chingford. Turn right along the main road to the Epping Forest Museum car park
Ordnance Survey maps	Landranger 177 (East London, Billericay, Gravesend), Explorer 174 (Epping Forest & Lee Valley)

The grassland, glades and splendid woodlands of Epping Forest, once part of the vast royal hunting-grounds of the Forest of Essex, are the setting for this walk. It takes you through an attractive and varied mixture of dense woodland and open grassland with some magnificent old trees and extensive views. As the forest is a public recreation area there are a multitude of paths and tracks but the absence of waymarking can cause confusion and make it difficult to stick to a precise route. For the most part this walk follows a clear and unambiguous route but there are places – especially in the vicinity of the Epping Forest Centre at High Beach – where the route directions need to be followed carefully.

During the Middle Ages the Forest of Essex, subsequently known as Waltham Forest, covered much of the county, and its proximity to the capital made it one of the most popular of royal hunting-grounds. From the 17th century onwards, fellings and enclosures caused it to shrink rapidly and it became fragmented. The present Epping Forest is the largest of the remaining frag-ments, covering nearly 6000 acres (2428ha), and was fortunately saved from further destruction by the Corporation of the City of London.

By an Act of Parliament in 1878, the Corporation became the Conservators of Epping Forest in order to preserve it 'as an open space for the recreation and enjoyment of the public'. In the 18th century, Epping Forest was a favourite haunt of the notorious highwayman Dick Turpin.

Queen Elizabeth's Hunting Lodge, at the start of the walk, was in fact built for Henry VIII as a grandstand from which to view the hunt. Since 1895 the lodge has functioned as the Epping Forest Museum.

Begin by turning right out of the car park and, just past a restaurant, turn left on to a path that keeps to the left of a small pool and heads downhill across the open grassland of Chingford Plain. There are fine views ahead over the forest. The route is marked by white posts with horseshoes to indicate that this path is also available to riders. On reaching a track at a bend **A**, bear left along it. This is the Green Ride, and you follow this clear, broad, sandy track through the forest for the next 1 1/2 miles (2.4km), ignoring all side turns. The Green Ride keeps in a fairly straight line but look out for a fork, where you take the left-hand track. After following the

Epping Forest

again. After about 100 yds (91m) and just before the track bears slightly left, look out for a path on the right that bears slightly left and descends to the busy A104, opposite a parking area **D**.

Cross the road and, at the end of the parking area, take the path on the right, at a Three Forests Way fingerpost, and follow it through another magnificent area of woodland (Little Monk Wood) to the earthworks of Loughton Camp, an ancient fortification. Keep along the right edge of the earthworks as they curve gradually to the left and continue past the camp, heading downhill and bearing left to reach a T-junction **E**. Turn right along a track – the Green Ride again – and follow it gently uphill to a road.

Cross over and continue along the track opposite, keeping to the left of a small pool. When you catch a glimpse of Strawberry Hill Pond on the right, turn right on to a path that keeps to the right of it to emerge into an open area. Bear left to follow the path across this open area into woodland again to a T-junction. Turn right on to a track and walk through a car park to the A104 again. Cross over, take the track opposite across another open area, cross a lane **F** and continue through woodland.

The track bears left. At a fork take the left-hand track, which later bears first left and then right and continues to a crossway. Turn left, here rejoining both the Green Ride and the outward route, and retrace your steps to the starting point. ●

track around right and left bends and keeping alongside an open area on the right, continue winding uphill through woodland to eventually emerge on to a road **B**.

Turn left and, just before the road forks, turn right through a fence gap and walk along a path – waymarked with horseshoe posts – that keeps parallel to the road that is signposted to High Beach and Epping. At a T-junction, turn left to the road and turn right along it to the King's Oak pub. Across the open area to the left is a fine view, with the tower of Waltham Abbey clearly visible.

Just beyond the pub, turn right **C** along a tarmac drive to the Epping Forest Centre – plenty of books, maps and guides here – and at the entrance, turn left on to a specially constructed wheelchair path. Immediately bear right alongside a fence on the right – broken down and incomplete in places – bearing right to a fence corner. Turn left here along a path through an outstandingly beautiful area of woodland and, on reaching a track, turn left

Biggin Hill

Start	Biggin Hill, Recreation Ground car park off Church Road
Distance	6½ miles (10.5km). Add ½ mile (800m) if coming by bus to Biggin Hill
Approximate time	3 hours (3¼ hours if coming by bus)
Parking	Recreation Ground car park at Biggin Hill
Refreshments	Pubs and cafés at Biggin Hill; pub at South Street
Public transport	Trains from London (Victoria) to Bromley South, bus to Biggin Hill (at time of printing no. 320) and walk along Church Road to the car park, which is on the left
Ordnance Survey maps	Landranger 187 (Dorking, Reigate & Crawley), Explorer 147 (Sevenoaks & Tonbridge)

The walk explores the well-wooded and gently rolling country of the North Downs to the south and east of Biggin Hill. A short stretch of the North Downs Way is used, and from the crest of the downs the views across to the Kent Weald are superb, despite the unavoidable sight and sounds of the M25 in the valley below. This is a well-waymarked route, following regular 'Berry's Green Circular Walk' signs.

Biggin Hill has left an indelible mark on British history as one of the airfields that played a vital role in the Battle of

Near Biggin Hill

Britain in 1940. The airport is just to the north of the village. Begin by turning left out of the car park along Church Road, turn left into Old Tye Avenue and immediately turn right along an

enclosed path, at a public footpath sign to Berry's Green. Keep ahead – in a more or less straight line – across or along the edge of a succession of fields and over a series of stiles, finally climbing a stile in a field corner on to a track.

Continue along this track, climb a stile on to a tarmac track and turn right Ⓐ in the South Street direction. The track becomes concrete, and where it bears right to the Foal Animal Rescue Centre, keep ahead along a tree-lined path by the right edge of a golf-course. After the path turns left, keep ahead across a field to the main road at South Street and turn left along it. At a public footpath sign to Knockholt, turn left along a drive Ⓑ and, in front of ornamental gates, bear right along an enclosed path.

Cross a track, keep ahead along another enclosed path, passing under a long green canopy, climb a stile, and another one immediately in front, and continue along an enclosed path. Cross a lane, climb the stile ahead, walk along the left edge of a field, by an inter- rupted hedge and line of trees on the left, and climb a stile in the field corner. Continue along an enclosed path, climb another stile and keep along the left edge of fields, climbing a series of stiles and heading down into a dip and up again. Finally walk across the middle of a field and climb a stile on to a lane.

Turn left and, at a public footpath sign, turn right Ⓒ along a track to the left of a farmhouse. The track becomes enclosed, descends through trees and curves left to join the North Downs Way. After climbing a stile, keep ahead along the top edge of a steeply sloping field and from the crest of the downs there is a superb and extensive view to the right looking across the Kentish Weald. Climb a stile, continue through a belt of trees, bearing left to climb another stile, and keep along the left

edge of a field. Follow the field edge to the right and, at a Berry's Green Circular Walk sign, turn left over a stile Ⓓ – here leaving the North Downs Way – and continue across the next field to a stile.

Climb it, keep ahead, passing to the left of a house, to the corner of a lane and continue along it – there is a duck pond on the left – to a T-junction. Turn left and almost immediately turn right along Bombers Lane. Where the tarmac lane ends, turn left along a track – Old Harrow Lane – which narrows to become an enclosed path and continues through the attractive Shellem Wood, heading steadily downhill. At the bottom, turn right over a stile Ⓔ at a public footpath sign to Cudham and

SCALE 1:25000 or 2½ INCHES to 1 MILE 4CM to 1KM

walk along the left edge of a field.
Climb a stile, continue through an area
of rough grassland, trees and bushes,
climb another stile and bear left to keep
along the top left edge of a field.

Continue – between trees on the left
and a wire fence on the right – to a stile,
climb it and keep ahead to climb a stile
on to a lane. Turn right and at a public
footpath sign to Berry's Green **F** turn
left up steps and over a stile and walk
along the right edge of a field. Climb a
stile into woodland, almost immediately
climb another and follow a well-
waymarked route through the wood to
join an obvious path. Continue along it,
turn left at a three-way fork and keep
along an undulating path to a lane.

Turn right, follow the lane around left
and right bends into Berry's Green and,
at a public footpath sign 'Berry's Green
Circular Walk, Short Walk', turn left
over a stile **G**.

Bear slightly left across a field to
climb a stile and keep ahead across the
next field, making for a stile in the far
left corner. Climb it and bear slightly
right to follow a straight, waymarked
route across a golf-course, heading
towards a footpath sign on the far side.
After crossing two drives and climbing
two stiles, pick up the outward route **A**
and retrace your steps to the start. ●

Esher Common, Oxshott Heath and West End Common

Start	West End Common (Horseshoe Clump car park), 1½ miles (2.4km) south of Esher on the A307
Distance	7 miles (11.3km). Add ½ mile (800m) if coming from Oxshott Station and pick up the walk at point **G**
Approximate time	3½ hours (3¾ hours from Oxshott Station)
Parking	Horseshoe Clump car park on West End Common
Refreshments	Pub at West End
Public transport	Trains from London (Waterloo) to Oxshott. Turn right along the station drive, turn left into the Oxshott Heath Visitors Car Park and pass beside a barrier to follow a track into woodland. Bear left on meeting another track to emerge into open grassland and at a public footpath sign to Fairmile, bear right and then right again on to a more obvious path. Re-enter woodland, head gently uphill to a path junction and turn sharp right up steps to join the main route at point **G**
Ordnance Survey maps	Landranger 176 (West London), Explorer 161 (London South, Croydon & Esher)

The three adjacent commons of Esher, West End and Oxshott Heath, collectively known as Elmbridge Commons, are remnants of the extensive heathlands that used to cover much of western Surrey. In the past such areas were regarded with horror by travellers but now they are seen as rare examples of a rural wilderness that needs to be zealously preserved. This figure-of-eight walk can easily be split into two separate shorter walks but the proliferation of paths and tracks across the commons requires you to follow the route directions carefully.

Facing the road, start by taking the path that leads off from the bottom right-hand corner of the car park, passing through a barrier. At a crossing of paths, turn left down to the road **A** cross it, pass between a barrier, at a public footpath sign to Oxshott Heath, and take a path through the woodlands of Esher Common, following a yellow-waymarked route.

Keep ahead at the first crossway and at the second one pass beside a barrier and continue along the right edge of the austere and mysterious-looking Black Pond. Pass beside another barrier on to a broad track, bear left, in the Oxshott

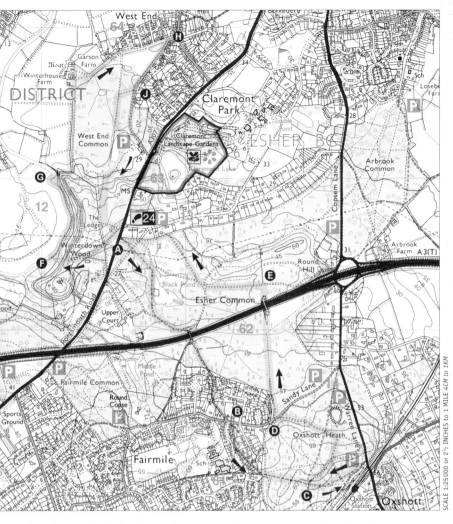

SCALE 1:25000 or 2½ INCHES to 1 MILE 4CM to 1KM

0	200	400	600	800 METRES	1
					KILOMETRES MILES
0	200	400	600 YARDS	½	

Heath direction, and the track becomes tarmacked, ascending and turning right to cross a bridge over the busy A3. At a public bridleway sign 'Horse Ride, Oxshott Heath', re-enter woodland, keep ahead at a public footpath sign and, at a fork by the next sign, take the right-hand path.

Pass under a barrier to continue along an enclosed path between fences, pass beside a barrier on to a road, turn left and almost immediately turn right **B** along another enclosed path. The path emerges briefly on to a road, bears

left and continues to the edge of Oxshott Heath. Bear left to a junction. Here a blue-waymarked post indicates a 'Horse Ride' on the right but the route keeps straight ahead across the heath, heading first uphill and then descending to a crossway **C**.

If returning to Oxshott Station, keep ahead to retrace your earlier route.

At the crossway, turn left to ascend steps and keep ahead along a ridge. From here there are grand views to the right across the heath. At a junction of paths by a war memorial, bear left on to a path that passes to the right of it – there is a white-waymarked Circular Walk post here – and at a crossway by

Oxshott Heath

another Circular Walk post, turn left, looking out for a Horse Ride sign on a tree trunk ahead. Take the left-hand path at a fork, which descends to a junction and a blue-waymarked Horse Ride post. Keep ahead along a path – there is another Horse Ride sign attached to a tree – which bears left to keep parallel with a road and at a Horse Ride post turn right to the road **D**.

Cross over, take the path opposite, signposted to Esher Common, which soon broadens out into a wide sandy track, and follow it in a straight line across the heath. It becomes a tarmac track that crosses the A3 and then reverts to a sandy track. At a crossway by a Horse Ride post, turn left **E**, continue to a junction (Five Ways) and turn half-right on to a path that has fencing ahead. Keep initially beside the fencing on the left and at a T-junction, turn left to continue along the right edge of the common. At a crossway, turn right to pick up the outward route and keep ahead through a barrier to the A307 **A**.

Cross over and continue through the trees of West End Common to a crossway. Horseshoe Clump car park is just to the right but the route continues to the left along a fairly straight and wide path to a T-junction. Turn left, take the first path on the right, pass

through a barrier and descend steps to the banks of the River Mole **F**. Turn right alongside the river – there are boardwalks in places – and at a footpath sign 'Steps and West End', turn right away from it **G** and ascend steps to pass beside another barrier. From here there are fine views over the Mole valley.

Pass a footpath post, bear slightly right along the left, inside edge of the common, and the path curves left to a T-junction. Turn left to keep along the left edge of the woodland to a barrier and beyond that continue along a tarmac drive. Pass under a metal barrier to the right of Winterhouse Farm, turn right at a T-junction and continue along a tarmac drive to emerge from the trees on to the edge of the large green at West End. This picturesque spot has all the ingredients that make up a tradi-tional English village green: pub, duck pond, cricket pitch and church. The latter is a small, white-painted corrugated iron structure built in 1879.

Walk along the left edge of the green, turn right **H** at the Prince of Wales pub, keep past the church and, after passing a pond on the right, turn right beside a barrier **J**, heading into woodland again. At a crossway, turn left along a straight path, with ditches both sides, turn left to cross a ditch, go up steps, pass through a fence gap and bear right to continue across rough grassland. The path curves left to a T-junction, where you turn right on to a clearer path, re-entering woodland.

Bear right to another T-junction in front of a mound, turn left along a path that bears right steeply uphill and keep ahead at the top. Bear left on joining another path and at a fork take the left-hand path to emerge into a clearing where there is a wooden carving of a dolphin. Turn left on to a path that heads downhill to the start. ●

Colne Valley, South Harefield and Bayhurst Wood

Start	Denham Country Park, Colne Valley Visitor Centre
Distance	7 miles (11.3km). Add 1½ miles (2.4km) if coming from Denham Station and pick up the walk at the bridge over the Grand Union Canal at South Harefield near point Ⓑ
Approximate time	3½ hours (4½ hours from Denham Station)
Parking	Denham Country Park
Refreshments	Pub by Widewater Lock; café at visitor centre
Public transport	Trains from London (Marylebone) to Denham. From the station platform, turn left under the tunnel, descend more steps and walk along a tarmac path to a lane. Turn left to a T-junction, turn right and follow the road to the canal bridge to join the main route near point Ⓑ
Ordnance Survey maps	Landranger 176 (West London), Explorer 172 (Chiltern Hills East, High Wycombe, Maidenhead)

From the pleasant environs of Denham Country Park, the route first follows the towpath of the Grand Union Canal to South Harefield. It then heads across to Bayhurst Wood, a remnant of the ancient Forest of Middlesex, and on the final leg you pass some pools created from gravel extraction, now an attractive feature of the Colne valley. The fine open views and rural nature of this walk convey something of the flavour of John Betjeman's largely vanished 'Rural Middlesex'. There may be mud in places.

Denham Country Park is part of the Colne Valley Regional Park. The latter, stretching along the western outskirts of London, was established in 1965 to make the Colne valley a greener and more attractive area and to improve its facilities for outdoor activities.

The walk begins in front of the visitor centre. Turn left along a path signposted 'Three Rivers Trail', between a car park on the left and the River Misbourne. Go through a gate, cross a road to the left of a bridge and go through the gate opposite. The path turns left away from the river to a crossing of paths.

Keep ahead along the bridleway, which runs along the right edge of woodland, curving right, and at a path junction and public bridleway sign turn left on to a track into the trees. The track bends right to cross a footbridge over the River Colne and continues winding through this attractive woodland. Shortly after a right bend, you reach a footpath sign to Denham Quarry. Turn right to the towpath of the Grand Union Canal and turn left on to it Ⓐ, passing under bridge 182. Follow the towpath for 1¼ miles (2km), going under a railway bridge and passing Harefield

Marina. In front of the first road bridge, bear left and climb steps to the road.

If returning to Denham Station, turn left here and retrace your outward route.

Turn right over the bridge by Widewater Lock and, after passing to the right of modern factory buildings, turn left on to a concrete path **B** that runs along the left edge of a recreation ground. The path later becomes enclosed between wire fences and emerges on to a road. Turn right and at a T-junction cross the main road, pass beside a metal gate, at a

public footpath sign, and take the gently ascending track ahead. In front of a metal gate, follow the track to the left, passing the Australian Military Cemetery on the right. Many Australian soldiers wounded in the Gallipoli landings in 1915 were sent to Harefield for hospital treatment and died from their wounds. The track emerges on to a tarmac drive by an attractive brick and flint church of medieval origin.

Walk along the drive as far as a Hillingdon Trail sign, turn right over a stile **C** and follow a path to another stile. Climb it, keep along an enclosed path, by the wall of the churchyard on the right, and continue through woodland, passing to the right of some stagnant pools and through a kissing-gate. Continue through trees and, after emerging from them at a Hillingdon Trail sign, bear left to climb a stile. Keep along the left edge of a field, don't climb the stile in the field corner but turn right along the left field edge – later by trees – to a stile at the corner of the woodland. Climb it, immediately turn left over another stile and walk along the right edge of woodland, heading downhill to a stile in the bottom corner of the field.

Climb the stile, turn left and then immediately right and follow a path through the trees to climb another stile. Continue along the right edge of woodland, and the path passes beside two fences to enter Bayhurst Wood Country Park. This highly attractive area of woodland, once part of the old Forest of Middlesex, mainly comprises oak, hornbeam, beech and sweet chestnut. Keep ahead near the left, inside edge of the wood, following Hillingdon Trail signs. After passing under a wooden arch, turn right **D** at the next Hillingdon Trail sign on to a wide path that continues through this beautiful area of woodland. Keep ahead on the main path all the while, descending to a crossing of paths and tracks on the far side of the wood and in front of a pond.

Don't turn left on to the track – there is a Hillingdon Trail sign here – but cross the track to the pond and then turn left on to a path that keeps along the right inside edge of the trees. Pass a picnic and barbecue area, continue to a T-junction and turn right along a winding track – this may be muddy in places – which emerges on to a lane. Turn right and, where the lane bends to the right, bear left **E** on to a track, at a public bridleway sign. This attractive, tree-lined track first ascends and then descends to reach a concrete drive. Keep ahead to a

The River Colne near Denham

road, turn right to pass under a railway bridge and, at a public footpath sign about 100 yds (91m) beyond, turn right along a tarmac drive to a stile **F**.

Climb the stile and continue along the drive, which turns left. Where the drive ends, climb the stile ahead – by a pond – and walk along the left edge of a field. The path, which later becomes enclosed, continues to a stile. Climb it, keep ahead through a belt of trees to climb another one and bear right along the right edge of the next field, by a hedge on the right. Climb a stile, head across a field, climb another stile on the far side and continue across the next field to climb a stile on to a road **G**.

Climb the stile opposite, continue across a field and climb two more stiles to reach the edge of a golf-course. Keep ahead to join a track and follow it gently downhill across the course. Continue through a belt of trees and, at a public footpath sign, turn right and walk across the grass, making for some trees. Follow a track through an area of trees and bushes, cross a causeway between two pools – these are some of the pools formed from flooded gravel pits – continue over a track and cross a footbridge over a stream.

Walk across another causeway and, on the far side, keep ahead to the canal. Cross the canal bridge **A** to rejoin the outward route back to the start. ●

Nonsuch Park and the Hogsmill River

Nonsuch Park and the Hogsmill River

Start	Ewell West Station
Distance	8½ miles (13.7km). Shorter version 4 miles (6.4km)
Approximate time	4½ hours (2 hours for shorter walk)
Parking	Ewell West Station
Refreshments	Pubs and cafés at Ewell; tearoom at Nonsuch Mansion
Public transport	Trains from London (Waterloo) to Ewell West
Ordnance Survey maps	Landranger 176 (West London), Explorer 161 (London South, Croydon & Esher)

The first part of the walk is basically a circuit of the highly attractive Nonsuch Park, site of a huge but now vanished palace built by Henry VIII. The shorter version returns directly to the start but the full walk continues through woodland and across narrow strips of meadowland beside the Hogsmill River, green fingers of countryside amidst a predominantly suburban landscape, to Tolworth Court Bridge. From there you retrace your steps beside the river, back to Ewell.

Emerging from the station, cross the road and take the enclosed path opposite. At the end of the path, turn left along a road to a T-junction and turn right into Lyncroft Gardens. At the next T-junction, keep ahead here along an enclosed tarmac path, cross a road, take the tree-lined path opposite and pass beside a barrier on to Ewell High Street.

Keep ahead along Reigate Road and, just before reaching Hazel Mead, turn left beside a barrier **A** and walk along a tree-lined drive. Turn right along Cheam Road, cross the busy dual carriageway, turn right and almost immediately turn left on to a hedge-and tree-lined path. Look out for a road on the left and turn along it **B**. Keep ahead at traffic lights along Nonsuch Court Avenue, which heads gently

uphill and later becomes Seymour Avenue. All the adjacent roads are named after the wives of Henry VIII.

Where the road ends, keep ahead through a fence gap – by a Woodland Trust sign and a London Loop footpath post – and continue across open grassland. The spire of Cheam church can be seen on the horizon. The path gently descends to a crossway, where you turn left **C** towards trees, crossing three tracks in quick succession to reach a tarmac drive. Turn right along it, here entering Nonsuch Park. The present park is only a remnant of the original extensive park, much of which is now covered by suburban housing, and there is hardly any trace of the huge palace built by Henry VIII in 1538. He modelled it on the contemporary palaces in France and Italy and

Approaching Nonsuch Park

described it as 'non pareil' (without equal, nothing like it – hence nonsuch). Charles II bestowed it on one of his mistresses, Barbara Villiers, Duchess of Cleveland, who had it demolished in the 1680s.

Just after passing beside a barrier **D**, turn left towards Nonsuch Mansion and turn left through a gate in a wall to walk along the back of the house. Follow the path to the right and right again and go through another gate to emerge in front of the house. Nonsuch Mansion – nothing to do with the vanished palace – was originally built in the 18th century but its present appearance is mainly the result of Wyatt's rebuilding and enlargement (1802–6).

From the front of the house, take the tarmac track that curves left and, just after emerging from the gardens, bear slightly right off the track and continue along a grassy path across the open expanses of the park. At a three-way fork, take the middle path and at a junction turn left along a straight, grassy path, by a line of trees on the left, to rejoin the tree-lined tarmac drive **E**.

Turn right and as you proceed the actual site of the palace is over to the right. At a fork by a small triangular green, take the left-hand path and at the next fork continue along the right-hand path through woodland. Turn right at a crossing of paths, by a concrete post No. 5 – the low wall to the left marks the site of the banqueting-house of the palace – and continue past post No. 6 to a London Loop footpath post. Turn left, continue along the right edge of trees and at the next post turn right to descend steps. Turn left to emerge on to the busy Ewell bypass, cross over and go through a hedge gap on the other side. Go down steps, continue along an enclosed path and turn right along a road, passing to the right of Ewell church to a T-junction **F**. The church

was built in 1848, and in the churchyard the Old Tower survives from its
medieval predecessor.

*For the short walk, turn left at the
T-junction, turn right at the traffic
lights across a causeway and follow
the curve of the road to the left. At a
T-junction, turn right into Chessington
Road to return to the start.*

For the full walk, turn left at **F**
then bear right along Mill Lane to a
T-junction. Turn right, immediately

turn left along a tarmac drive, at a sign
to Upper Mill, and after crossing a
bridge over the narrow Hogsmill River,
turn right – there is a London Loop
footpath post here – on to a path
alongside the river. At the next London
Loop post, turn right to cross two
streams, continue through attractive
woodland and turn left on to a board-
walk above the middle of the river that
takes you under a railway bridge to a
T-junction.

Turn first right and then left to
continue along the right bank of the
river, across a mixture of meadows,

to keep alongside the ornamental lake, keep ahead at a crossway and at a fork take the right-hand path, which curves right and goes through a metal gate to another T-junction.

Continue alongside the Hogsmill River for about 1 mile (1.6km) to Tolworth Court Bridge, mainly along narrow strips of attractive meadowland, tree-lined in places. At one stage you cross a main road. On reaching the bridge, turn left over it and, on the other side, turn left again **H** at a public footpath sign 'Hogsmill Walk, Tolworth Court Farm'. Go through a fence gap, walk along the left edge of a rough meadow and turn left over a stile **J**. Descend steps to cross first stepping-stones over Bonesgate Stream and then a metal footbridge over the river.

Turn right, here picking up the outward route, and retrace your steps to where you rejoined the river after emerging from Ewell Court. Turn right, at a London Loop post, to cross the Hogsmill River for the last time and turn left to follow a path along its right bank. At the next footbridge, turn right **K** along a tarmac path, by a high wire fence bordering a recreation ground on the right, and continue along a drive between houses to a road. Bear left along Northcroft Road to a T-junction, turn right and immediately turn left to cross a bridge over a stream.

Take the first turning on the left and where the road ends turn right along the right edge of a meadow. Turn right along the next road, turn left on to an enclosed tarmac path **L** and cross a footbridge over the railway line. Continue to a road, walk along it, turning first left and then right, to reach a T-junction and turn right. Follow the curve of the road to the left and at a T-junction, turn right along Chessington Road to return to the starting point. ●

woodland, rough grass and scrub, following the regular London Loop waymarks. It is hard to believe that this placid valley was a centre for gunpowder manufacture from Elizabethan times up to as late as the 1860s; there were several powder mills along the river. On reaching a footbridge, don't cross it but turn right alongside the grounds of Ewell Court on the left. About 50 yds (46m) before a T-junction, bear left through a metal gate into the grounds **G**, now a delightful public park, and the tarmac path bends left to a T-junction. Turn left

Farthing Downs and Happy Valley

Farthing Downs and Happy Valley

Start	Farthing Downs, first car park on Downs Road ½ mile (800m) south of Coulsdon South Station
Distance	8 miles (12.9km). Add 1 mile (1.6km) if coming from Coulsdon South Station
Approximate time	4 hours (4½ hours from Coulsdon South Station)
Parking	Farthing Downs
Refreshments	Kiosk in second car park near point Ⓐ
Public transport	Trains from London (Victoria, Waterloo East and Charing Cross) to Coulsdon South. Turn right and, where the Station Forecourt curves left, bear right along a tarmac path. Descend steps to Marlpit Lane, turn right under a bridge, take the second road on the right (Downs Road) and head uphill on to Farthing Downs to the first car park for the start
Ordnance Survey maps	Landranger 187 (Dorking, Reigate & Crawley), Explorer 146 (Dorking, Box Hill & Reigate)

This scenic and fairly energetic walk on the downs to the south of Croydon embraces a series of woodlands, the beautiful chalk meadowland of the secluded Happy Valley and grand views over the North Downs. It also passes the isolated medieval church at Chaldon and includes a stretch of the North Downs Way. The route is well-waymarked with 'Downlands Circular Walk' signs.

Farthing Downs, one of four commons near Coulsdon, is one of a number of areas of open country on the outskirts of the capital that are owned by the Corporation of the City of London. It has been maintained by the Corporation as a public recreation area since 1883.

From the car park, turn left along the lane – or alternatively along one of the four parallel paths, two each side of the lane – that runs along the ridge of Farthing Downs to the next car park. Approaching the car park, head across the grass to a large Farthing Downs information board and beyond that turn right on to a path Ⓐ at a public footpath sign to Devilsden Wood and Happy Valley. Pass beside a metal barrier to enter the sloping woodland.

At a fork, take the left-hand lower path, signposted to Happy Valley, continue through Devilsden Wood and, on emerging from it, keep ahead along the top right edge of the chalk grassland of Happy Valley. In the field corner – at a public footpath sign to Chaldon church – turn half-right into trees, bear left and continue along the right edge of grassland to the next field corner.

0	200	400	600	800 METRES	1	
						KILOMETRES
						MILES
0	200	400	600 YARDS		½	

SCALE 1:25000 or 2½ INCHES to 1 MILE 4CM to 1KM

Happy Valley

Turn right **B**, head uphill through a narrow belt of trees and continue more or less in a straight line across two fields. Re-enter woodland, head up to a lane, turn left and at a fork, take the right lane to pass to the left of Chaldon church. This beautiful little flint church, which dates back to the 12th century, possesses one of the earliest-known wall-paintings in England. The broach spire was not added until 1842.

Just after passing the church, turn left **C** over a stile, at a public footpath sign to Alderstead Heath, and walk across a field to climb another stile. Bear slightly right along the right edge of the next field but, before reaching the field corner, the path bears left across to a stile. Climb it, keep in the same direction across the next field and, at a hedge corner, bear right along the right field edge and turn right over a stile into Furzefield Wood.

Keep ahead to cross a track, go along a concrete track, pass between upright posts and at a crossway turn left in the Dean Lane direction. Where the track bears right, keep ahead along a path to climb a stile, turn right and then left to walk along the right edge of a field – parallel to Dean Lane – and turn right through a kissing-gate on to the lane **D**. Cross over, take the concrete drive ahead to Tollsworth Manor Farm, and just past it turn left along a track into a field.

Turn right along the right field edge, go through a hedge gap, and ahead is a fine view over the North Downs. The built-up area on the opposite slopes is Redhill and Reigate. Turn left along the top field edge **E** and continue along an enclosed, hedge-lined path, here joining the North Downs Way. Cross Hilltop Lane, take the track ahead, passing some large houses, and continue along an enclosed path into woodland. Keep along the right-hand path at a junction and look out for a public footpath sign to Rook Lane, where you leave the North Downs Way by turning left to a stile **F**.

Climb the stile, walk along an enclosed path by woodland on the left and at a junction of five ways, keep ahead over a stile and continue along an enclosed path. After climbing the next stile, turn first right and then left, pass to the right of Rook Farm and climb another stile on to a road. Take the lane ahead (Doctors Lane) and after ¼ mile (400m), turn right into Leazes Avenue **G**. Continue along the left edge of a green at a fork and keep ahead along a track.

At a public bridleway sign to Happy Valley in front of gates, continue along a path through Piles Wood, heading gently downhill to emerge from the trees at the southern end of Happy Valley. At a footpath post, turn left **H** through a hedge gap, in the Happy Valley direction, and walk along a springy, grassy path through the valley, a narrow belt of chalk grassland between gently sloping woodland. Keep ahead all the while, following signs to Farthing Downs – passing through first a hedge gap and then a belt of trees – and, a few yards before reaching a stony track, bear left **J** to cross a grassy track and head uphill through an area of grassland, trees and bushes.

At a crossway turn left, bear right and then bear left along a track, between blue-waymarked posts, up to Downs Road. Turn right and retrace your steps to the start. ●

Cudham and Downe

Start	High Elms Country Park
Distance	8 miles (12.9km)
Approximate time	4 hours
Parking	High Elms Country Park
Refreshments	Pub at Cudham; pubs and café at Downe, tearoom at Down House; refreshments at High Elms golf club
Public transport	Trains from London (Victoria) to Bromley South, bus 146 to Downe and pick up the walk by the church in Downe village
Ordnance Survey maps	Landrangers 177 (East London, Billericay & Gravesend) and 178 (Dorking, Reigate & Crawley), Explorer 147 (Sevenoaks & Tonbridge)

From High Elms Country Park the route proceeds through woodland and across fields to Cudham. It continues to Downe, passing Charles Darwin's house, and returns to the start by way of tracks and field paths. Both villages have fine medieval churches, and there are splendid views extending from the Thames basin to the North Downs. It is quite an energetic walk but well waymarked as most of it follows the frequent 'Cudham Circular Walk' signs.

High Elms Country Park is based on the former estate of the Lubbock family. Sir John William Lubbock built the house and laid out the grounds in the Italian style in the 1840s. In 1938 the estate passed into local authority ownership and, although the house was burnt down in 1967, the formal gardens and stables remain.

At the far end of the car park, turn right beside a barrier on to a tarmac track and, at a crossway and London Loop post, turn right to follow a curving track uphill through the ornamental gardens. Pass beside another barrier, bear left and, where the tarmac track ends, turn right across the grass and continue between hedges to a kissing-gate. Go through, walk through the car park of the High Elms golf club to a lane and turn left.

Just after passing the unusual High Elms Clockhouse, turn left on to a track **A** at a public bridleway sign to Cudham Lane North and continue along an enclosed, fence-lined path across the golf-course to enter Cuckoo Wood. Turn right beside a barrier to continue through this beautiful woodland, turn left at a crossway, turn left again at a T-junction and head downhill. Where the path curves left, turn right, at a yellow waymark, to continue downhill, keep ahead at a crossway and continue to a barrier. Pass under it, keeping ahead uphill along the right edge of a field. In the field corner turn right through a metal kissing-gate on to a lane **B**.

Turn right and then immediately left along Snag Lane. Where the lane turns right, keep ahead along an enclosed path, at a public bridleway sign to

SCALE 1:27 777 or about 2¼ INCHES to 1 MILE 3.6CM to 1KM

| 0 | 200 | 400 | 600 | 800 METRES | 1 |
| 0 | 200 | 400 | 600 YARDS | ½ | KILOMETRES MILES |

Knockholt and Pratt's Bottom. Descend under a canopy of trees and follow a curving and undulating path to a T-junction **C**. Turn right through a belt of trees and continue along the right edge of a field – later the path becomes a concrete one. After passing to the left of cottages and a farm, keep ahead along a lane that curves right. At a

public footpath sign to Cudham church, turn left over a stile.

As you continue along an enclosed path, there are distant views to the right of the Thames basin, with the tower blocks of the East End and the tower of Canary Wharf clearly visible. The path continues diagonally across a field to a stile. Climb it, head across the next field and on the far side go through a metal kissing-gate. Cross a tarmac drive, go through another metal kissing-gate and turn right along the right edge of a playing-field. There is a fine view of Cudham church ahead as you follow the edge of the playing-field to the left to a public footpath sign. This delightful flint church, small but quite wide, dates back to the 12th century and is unusual in that the central tower is on the south side.

Continue along a tarmac path by the field edge, pass beside a barrier into a car park and turn right to a lane **D**. Turn right and, opposite the Blacksmiths Arms, turn left over a stile, at a public footpath sign to Biggin Hill, and bear right downhill across a field to climb another stile. Continue steeply downhill through trees, climb a stile and turn left along a lane. Head down into a dip, then continue gently uphill and at a public footpath sign to Luxted and Downe **E**, bear right through a metal gate and head steeply uphill along a tree-lined tarmac drive. At a yellow waymark, turn right up steps, climb a stile and continue along an enclosed path that turns left and continues uphill. Bear right along a track to a road and turn right through Single Street.

At a public footpath sign by a right bend, turn left **F** in the Biggin Hill direction, along a narrow, enclosed path, follow it around left- and right-hand bends and continue to a stile. Climb it, turn right along the right edge of a field, climb another stile and continue along an enclosed path to a stile. Climb that one, keep ahead along a track to a lane, turn left and, where the lane bends right, keep ahead downhill along a tree-lined tarmac track.

Turn right **G**, at a public footpath sign to Downe, go past a post and walk along a hedge- and tree-lined path. The path continues first along the left edge of a field, then through woodland, then along the right edge of a golf-course and re-enters trees to reach a crossway. Turn right, in the Downe direction, and

head uphill – via steps – to a stile. Climb it and continue uphill, curving left and crossing a field to climb another stile.

For walkers who wish to visit Down House, turn right through a gate, turn left through another gate and walk through the grounds to the house. This was for 40 years the home of Charles Darwin, and visitors can see the study in which he worked and where he wrote *On the Origin of Species by Natural Selection* in 1859.

After climbing the stile, the route continues along an enclosed path to a lane. Turn right along it to a road and turn left **H** into the village of Downe, which has some attractive flint cottages, two pubs and a 13th-century church. *Those coming by bus join and leave the walk at this point.* The road curves left in the village centre and about $^1/_2$ mile (800m) further on – where the road bears left – turn right **J**, at a public footpath sign to Farnborough, on to a tree-lined and enclosed path that bears left and continues to a waymarked post. Pass beside it to walk along the left edge of a field and, at the next post, turn left through a wide hedge gap and continue across the next field to a stile.

Climb it, cross a track, take the enclosed path opposite and, at a junction of paths, turn sharp right up steps **K** – here rejoining the London Loop – and turn left along the left edge of a field. Descend steps in the field corner, turning left down to an enclosed track, and turn right along it to a lane. Turn left and, at a public footpath sign to High Elms, turn right **L** along an enclosed, uphill, tree-lined path.

Continue past two barriers, keep ahead through another belt of delightful woodland and the path descends across part of the High Elms golf-course again to a lane opposite the Clockhouse **A**. Turn left and retrace your steps through the Country Park to the start. ●

Further Information

 ## *The National Trust*

Anyone who likes visiting places of natural beauty and/or historic interest has cause to be grateful to the National Trust. Without it, many such places would probably have vanished by now.

It was in response to the pressures on the countryside posed by the relentless march of Victorian industrialisation that the trust was set up in 1895. Its founders, inspired by the common goals of protecting and conserving Britain's national heritage and widening public access to it, were Sir Robert Hunter, Octavia Hill and Canon Rawnsley: respectively a solicitor, a social reformer and a clergyman. The latter was particularly influential. As a canon of Carlisle Cathedral and vicar of Crosthwaite (near Keswick), he was concerned about threats to the Lake District and had already been active in protecting footpaths and promoting public access to open countryside. After the flooding of Thirlmere in 1879 to create a large reservoir, he became increasingly convinced that the only effective way to guarantee protection was outright ownership of land.

The purpose of the National Trust is to preserve areas of natural beauty and sites of historic interest by acquisition, holding them in trust for the nation and making them available for public access and enjoyment. Some of its properties have been acquired through purchase, but many have come to the Trust as donations. Nowadays, it is not only one of the biggest landowners in the country, but also one of the most active conservation charities, protecting 581,113 acres (253,176 ha) of land, including 555 miles (892km) of coastline, and over 300 historic properties in England, Wales and Northern Ireland. (There is a separate National Trust for Scotland, which was set up in 1931.)

Furthermore, once a piece of land has come under National Trust ownership, it is difficult for its status to be altered. As a result of parliamentary legislation in 1907, the Trust was given the right to declare its property inalienable, so ensuring that in any subsequent dispute it can appeal directly to parliament.

As it works towards its dual aims of conserving areas of attractive countryside and encouraging greater public access (not easy to reconcile in this age of mass tourism), the Trust provides an excellent service for walkers by creating new concessionary paths and waymarked trails, maintaining stiles and footbridges and combating the ever-increasing problem of footpath erosion.

For details of membership, contact the National Trust at the address on page 95.

 ## *The Ramblers' Association*

No organisation works more actively to protect and extend the rights and interests of walkers in the countryside than the Ramblers' Association. Its aims are clear: to foster a greater knowledge, love and care of the countryside; to assist in the protection and enhancement of public rights of way and areas of natural beauty; to work for greater public access to the countryside; and to encourage more people to take up rambling as a healthy, recreational leisure activity.

It was founded in 1935 when, following the setting up of a National Council of Ramblers' Federations in 1931, a number of federations earlier formed in London, Manchester, the Midlands and elsewhere came together to create a more effective pressure group, to deal with such problems as the disappearance and obstruction of footpaths, the prevention of access to open mountain and moorland and increasing hostility from landowners. This was the era of the mass trespasses, when there were sometimes violent confrontations between ramblers and

The modern face of St Katharine Docks

gamekeepers, especially on the moorlands of the Peak District.

Since then the Ramblers' Association has played an influential role in preserving and developing the national footpath network, supporting the creation of national parks and encouraging the designation and waymarking of long-distance routes.

Our freedom to walk in the countryside is precarious and requires constant vigilance. As well as the perennial problems of footpaths being illegally obstructed, disappearing through lack of use or extinguished by housing or road construction, new dangers can spring up at any time.

It is to meet such problems and dangers that the Ramblers' Association exists and represents the interests of all walkers. The address to write to for information on the Ramblers' Association and how to become a member is given on page 95.

 ## Walkers and the Law

The average walker in a national park or other popular walking area, armed with the appropriate Ordnance Survey map, reinforced perhaps by a guidebook giving detailed walking instructions, is unlikely to run into legal difficulties, but it is useful to know something about the law relating to public rights of way. The right to walk over certain parts of the countryside has developed over a long period, and how such rights came into being is a complex subject, too lengthy to be discussed here. The following comments are intended simply as a helpful guide, backed up by the Countryside Access Charter, a concise summary of walkers' rights and obligations drawn up by the Countryside Commission (see page 92).

Basically there are two main kinds of public rights of way: footpaths (for walkers only) and bridleways (for walkers,

Further Information

Countryside Access Charter

Your rights of way are:

- public footpaths – on foot only. Sometimes waymarked in yellow
- bridle-ways – on foot, horseback and pedal cycle. Sometimes waymarked in blue
- byways (usually old roads), most 'roads used as public paths' and, of course, public roads – all traffic has the right of way

Use maps, signs and waymarks to check rights of way. Ordnance Survey Pathfinder and Landranger maps show most public rights of way

On rights of way you can:

- take a pram, pushchair or wheelchair if practicable
- take a dog (on a lead or under close control)
- take a short route round an illegal obstruction or remove it sufficiently to get past

You have a right to go for recreation to:

- public parks and open spaces – on foot
- most commons near older towns and cities – on foot and sometimes on horseback
- private land where the owner has a formal agreement with the local authority

In addition you can use the following by local or established custom or consent, but ask for advice if you are unsure:

- many areas of open country, such as moorland, fell and coastal areas, especially those in the care of the National Trust, and some commons
- some woods and forests, especially those owned by the Forestry Commission
- country parks and picnic sites
- most beaches
- canal towpaths
- some private paths and tracks Consent sometimes extends to horse-riding and cycling

For your information:

- county councils and London boroughs maintain and record rights of way, and register commons
- obstructions, dangerous animals, harassment and misleading signs on rights of way are illegal and you should report them to the county council
- paths across fields can be ploughed, but must normally be reinstated within two weeks
- landowners can require you to leave land to which you have no right of access
- motor vehicles are normally permitted only on roads, byways and some 'roads used as public paths'

riders on horseback and pedal cyclists). Footpaths and bridleways are shown by broken green lines on Ordnance Survey Pathfinder and Outdoor Leisure maps and broken red lines on Landranger maps. There is also a third category, called byways: chiefly broad tracks (green lanes) or farm roads, which walkers, riders and cyclists have to share, usually only occasionally, with motor vehicles. Many of these public paths have been in existence for hundreds of years and some even originated as prehistoric trackways and have been in constant use for well over 2000 years. Ways known as RUPPs (roads used as public paths) still appear on some maps. The legal definition of such byways is ambiguous and they are

gradually being reclassified as footpaths, bridleways or byways.

The term 'right of way' means exactly what it says. It gives right of passage over what, in the vast majority of cases, is private land, and you are required to keep to the line of the path and not stray on to the land on either side. If you inadvertently wander off the right of way – either because of faulty map-reading or because the route is not clearly indicated on the ground – you are technically trespassing and the wisest course is to ask the nearest available person (farmer or fellow walker) to direct you back to the correct route. There are stories about unpleasant confrontations between walkers and farmers at times, but in general most farmers are co-operative when responding to a genuine and polite request for assistance in route-finding.

Obstructions can sometimes be a problem and probably the most common of these is where a path across a field has been ploughed up. It is legal for a farmer to plough up a path provided that he restores it within two weeks, barring exceptionally bad weather. This does not always happen and here the walker is presented with a dilemma: to follow the line of the path, even if this inevitably means treading on crops, or to walk around the edge of the field. The latter course of action often seems the best but this means that you would be trespassing and not keeping to the exact line of the path. In the case of other obstructions which may block a path (illegal fences and locked gates etc), common sense has to be used in order to negotiate them by the easiest method – detour or removal. You should only ever remove as much as is necessary to get through, and if you can easily go round the obstruction without causing any damage, then you should do so. If you have any problems negotiating rights of way, you should report the matter to the rights of way department of the relevant council, which will take action with the landowner concerned.

Apart from rights of way enshrined by law, there are a number of other paths available to walkers. Permissive or concessionary paths have been created where a landowner has given permission for the public to use a particular route across his land. The main problem with these is that, as they have been granted as a concession, there is no legal right to use them and therefore they can be extinguished at any time. In practice, many of these concessionary routes have been established on land owned either by large public bodies such as the Forestry Commission, or by a private one, such as the National Trust, and as these mainly encourage walkers to use their paths, they are unlikely to be closed unless a change of ownership occurs.

Walkers also have free access to country parks (except where requested to keep away from certain areas for ecological reasons, eg wildlife protection, woodland regeneration, safeguarding of rare plants etc), canal towpaths and most beaches. By custom, though not by right, you may generally walk across the open and uncultivated higher land of mountain, moorland and fell, but this varies from area to area and from one season to another – grouse moors, for example, will be out of bounds during the breeding and shooting seasons and some open areas are used as Ministry of Defence firing ranges, so access will be restricted. In some areas

Exterior of the circular nave of Temple Church, completed in 1185

Further Information

the situation has been clarified as a result of 'access agreements' between the land-owners and either the county council or the national park authority, which clearly define when and where you can walk over such open country.

Walking Safety

Although the reasonably gentle country-side that is the subject of this book offers no real dangers to walkers at any time of the year, it is still advisable to take sensible precautions and follow certain well-tried guidelines.

Always take with you both warm and waterproof clothing and sufficient food and drink. Wear suitable footwear, such as strong walking-boots or shoes that give a good grip over stony ground, on slippery slopes and in muddy conditions. Try to obtain a local weather forecast and bear it in mind before you start. Do not be afraid to abandon your proposed route and return to your starting point in the event of unexpected bad weather.

All the walks described in this book will be safe to do, given due care and respect, even during the winter. Indeed, a crisp, fine winter day often provides perfect walking conditions, with firm ground underfoot and a clarity that is not possible to achieve at any other time of the year.

The most difficult hazard likely to be encountered is mud, especially when walking along woodland and field paths, farm tracks and bridleways – the latter in particular can often get churned up by cyclists and horses. In summer, an additional difficulty may be narrow and overgrown paths, particularly along the edges of cultivated fields. Neither should constitute a major problem provided that the appropriate footwear is worn.

Useful Organisations

(NB New London telephone numbers: From 22 April 2000 the new eight-digit number operates, which means that 0171 becomes 020 7, and 0181 becomes 020 8.)

British Travel Centre
Piccadilly Circus, London
(personal callers only)

Council for the Protection of Rural England
25 Buckingham Palace Road, London SW1W 0PP.
Tel. 0171 976 6433

Countryside Commission
John Dower House,
Crescent Place, Cheltenham,
Gloucestershire GL50 3RA.
Tel. 01242 521381

The dome of St Paul's from the South Bank of the Thames

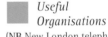

Downland near Cudham

English Heritage
23 Savile Row, London W1X 1AB.
Tel. 0171 973 3000

Forestry Commission
Information Branch, 231 Corstorphine Rd,
Edinburgh EH12 7AT.
Tel. 0131 334 0303

London Tourist Board
26 Grosvenor Gardens,
London SW1W 0DU.
Tel. 0171 932 2000
Tourist information centres:
Bexley: 0181 303 9052
Canary Wharf: 0171 512 9800
Croydon: 0181 253 1009
Foots Cray: 0181 300 4700
Greenwich: 0181 858 6376
Harrow: 0181 424 1102/3
Hillingdon: 01895 250706
Hounslow: 0181 572 8279
Islington: 0171 278 8787
Kingston Upon Thames: 0181 547 5592
Lewisham: 0181 297 8317
Redbridge: 0181 478 3020
Richmond: 0181 940 9125
Southwark: 0171 403 8299
Tower Hamlets: 0171 375 2549
Twickenham: 0181 891 1411

Long Distance Walkers' Association
21 Upcroft, Windsor, Berkshire SL4 3NH.
Tel. 01753 866685

National Trust
Membership and general enquiries:
PO Box 39, Bromley, Kent BR1 3XL.
Tel. 0181 315 1111

Thames and Chilterns Regional Office:
Hughenden Manor, High Wycombe,
Bucks. HP14 4LA. Tel. 01494 528051

Ordnance Survey
Romsey Road, Maybush,
Southampton SO16 4GU.
Tel. 08456 05 05 05 (Lo-call)

Ramblers' Association
1–5 Wandsworth Road, London SW8 2XX.
Tel. 0171 582 6878

Youth Hostels Association
8 St Stephen's Hill, St Albans, Herts.
AL1 2DY. Tel. 01727 855215

Ordnance Survey Maps for In and Around London

The area of *In and Around London* is covered by Ordnance Survey 1:50 000 ($1\frac{1}{4}$ inches to 1 mile or 2 cm to 1km) scale Landranger map sheets 166, 167, 176, 177, 187 and 188. These all-purpose maps are packed with information to help you explore the area and show viewpoints, picnic sites, places of interest and caravan and camping sites.

To examine the *In and Around London* area in more detail and especially if you are planning walks, Ordnance Survey Explorer maps at 1:25 000 ($2\frac{1}{2}$ inches to 1 mile or 4cm to 1km) scale are ideal:

146 Dorking, Box Hill & Reigate
147 Sevenoaks & Tonbridge
161 London South
162 Greenwich & Gravesend
172 Chiltern Hills East
173 London North
174 Epping Forest & Lee Valley

To get to the *In and Around London* area use the Ordnance Survey Great Britain Routeplanner Map (Travelmaster map number 1) at 1:625 000 (1 inch to 10 miles or 1cm to 6.25 km) scale or Travelmaster map 9 (South East England including London) at 1:250 000 (1 inch to 4 miles or 1cm to 2.5km) scale.

Ordnance Survey maps and guides are available from most booksellers, stationers and newsagents.

Further Information

Index

Entries in *italic type* refer to illustrations